PORTRAIT SERIES

GW00671489

98/99
SURREY LIBR
TRA/3

Narrow Gauge ... and ... Railway

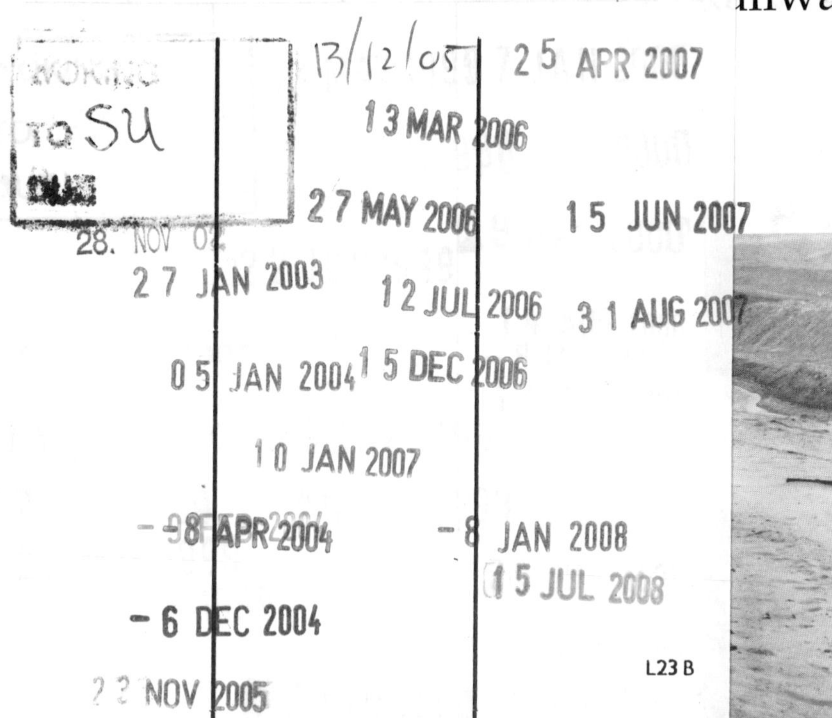

WOKING LIBRARY 01483 770591

WOKING TO SU

28. NOV 02
27 JAN 2003
05 JAN 2004
-8 APR 2004
-6 DEC 2004
22 NOV 2005
13/12/05
13 MAR 2006
27 MAY 2006
12 JUL 2006
15 DEC 2006
10 JAN 2007
25 APR 2007
15 JUN 2007
31 AUG 2007
-8 JAN 2008
15 JUL 2008

L23 B

SURREY COUNTY COUNCIL
Community Services

Charges will be payable at the Adult rate if this item is not returned by the latest date stamped above.

L21B

...S

© Oakwood Press & Rod Dingwall 1997

British Library Cataloguing in Publication Data
A Record for this book is available from the British Library
ISBN 0 85361 508 X

Typeset by Oakwood Graphics.
Repro by Ford Graphics, Ringwood, Hants.
Printed by D. Brown & Sons Ltd, Bridgend, Mid Glamorgan.

All rights reserved. No part of this book may be reproduced or transmitted in any form or by any means, electronic or mechanical, including photocopying, recording or by any information storage and retrieval system, without permission from the Publisher in writing.

Tracks in the Sand

I Dreamt that I was walking through a desert with God
And across the sky flashed past scenes from my life.
For each scene I noticed two sets of footprints in the sand
One belonged to me, the other to God.
When the last pictures of my life had disappeared
I looked back at the tracks in the sand, and noticed,
That at various times along the path of my life
There was only one set of footprints
I also realised that this occurred
At the lowest and saddest times of my life
This really troubled me and I asked God about it.
God, you said that once I decided to follow you
You would walk with me all the way but I can see
That during the most difficult times in my life
There is only one set of tracks in the sand
I don't understand, why, in times when
I needed you the most did you leave me.
God replied 'My precious child, I love you and would never never leave you
Especially during your times of trials and suffering
When you saw only one set of footprints in the sand
It was then that I carried you'.

Adapted from 'Footprints in the Sand' - Anon.

Cover Photographs
Front, above: Garside's locomotives *Red Rum* and *Damredub* doubleheading a train at Munday's Hill Quarry. *Front, below*: Arnold's dragline loads a train of skips in Nine Acre Quarry. *Rear, above*: Arnold's Simplexes on the tipping dock at New Trees Quarry. *Rear, below*: Garside's locomotive *Damredub* on its way to Churchways Quarry.

(All) Chris Battye

Title page: Track leading down to the lower greensand beds at Leighton Buzzard.

Author's Collection

Published by
The Oakwood Press
P.O. Box 122, Headington, Oxford OX3 8LU

Contents

A scene similar to the author's first encounter with the narrow gauge railway at Leighton Buzzard. *Pixie* crosses Shenley Hill Road with the aid of a flag man in 1970.

The Late John Brotherhood

Introduction

It was several months after moving to Leighton Buzzard that I discovered the narrow gauge railway. Whilst driving towards the centre of town I was signalled to stop at a level crossing by a man clad in oily overalls and wearing a grease top cap. He held up a grubby red flag. I came to a halt, not knowing quite what to expect. Moments later a loud, sharp, blast of a whistle pierced the air, and through a hiss of escaping steam emerged . . . *Pixie*. The vintage locomotive passed in front of me hauling rocking carriages full of waving, smiling passengers. She departed leaving a trail of smoke behind her.

The scene brought back fond memories of my childhood and so it was that I found myself heading towards the narrow gauge railway station where I too could join the train. Like so many visitors to the line before me the above apparition was my first introduction to what must be, until quite recently, one of the most undocumented of Britain's preserved railways. The purchase of a guide book at the station informed me that when I thought steam had finished in the late 1960s a group of enthusiasts had had different ideas. With a local sand company's permission they had taken over the use of the track to run their own engines at weekends. As I read further I was amazed to learn that the railway was originally built in 1919 and had initially carried thousands of tons of sand.

After travelling on the train I became eager to discover more information of the line at Leighton Buzzard and its origins. What followed was a decade of research, during which I have managed to collect many old and interesting photographs. When put together the images form an important record of our industrial heritage, they depict a story of days long ago and how the passage of time changes life so much. The pictures selected relate to the background surrounding the sand industry in Leighton Buzzard, and how the formation of the narrow gauge line came about. After construction of the Light Railway the photographs depict its route and show the locomotives and rolling stock that operated over the system up to its decline.

Today's railway enthusiasts who struggled to preserve the narrow gauge line in the early days can be pleased with their efforts. They have opened the line for passengers using restored vintage steam and diesel locomotives. There were many problems to be overcome, but happily in 1992 the Leighton Buzzard Narrow Gauge Railway celebrated its 25th anniversary, which was an amazing event featuring many visiting steam engines from all over the country.

During 1994 the 75th anniversary of the Leighton Buzzard Light Railway was celebrated; over this period more than 200 individual 2 ft gauge locomotives coming from an extremely wide variety of manufacturers have operated over the system.

I hope you will treasure and enjoy *Narrow Gauge Tracks in the Sand* as my contribution to the history of the line.

A further book telling the story of the 25 years of the preservation of the line by the Leighton Buzzard Narrow Gauge Railway Society is currently in preparation.

Rod Dingwall
Leighton Buzzard

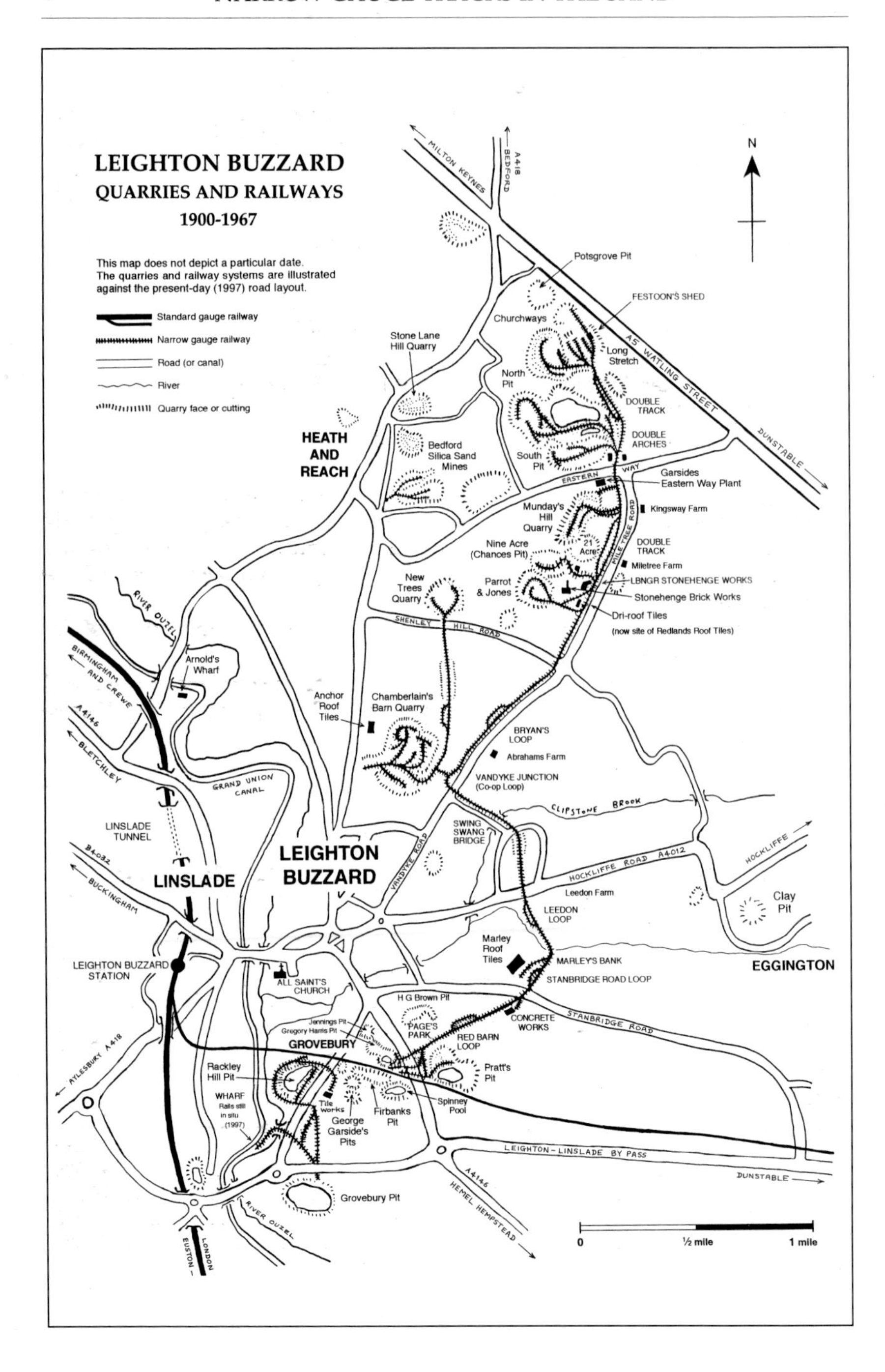
LEIGHTON BUZZARD
QUARRIES AND RAILWAYS
1900-1967
This map does not depict a particular date.
The quarries and railway systems are illustrated against the present-day (1997) road layout.
Standard gauge railway
Narrow gauge railway
Road (or canal)
River
Quarry face or cutting
N
Potsgrove Pit
FESTOON'S SHED
Churchways
Long Stretch
North Pit
DOUBLE TRACK
DOUBLE ARCHES
South Pit
Garsides Eastern Way Plant
Kingsway Farm
Munday's Hill Quarry
Nine Acre (Chances Pit)
21 Acre
DOUBLE TRACK
Miletree Farm
LBNGR STONEHENGE WORKS
Stonehenge Brick Works
Parrot & Jones
Dri-roof Tiles
(now site of Redlands Roof Tiles)
Stone Lane Hill Quarry
Bedford Silica Sand Mines
HEATH AND REACH
New Trees Quarry
SHENLEY HILL ROAD
EASTERN WAY
MILETREE ROAD
A5 WATLING STREET
DUNSTABLE
MILTON KEYNES
A418 BEDFORD
RIVER OUZEL
Arnold's Wharf
BIRMINGHAM AND CREWE
A4146
BLETCHLEY
Anchor Roof Tiles
Chamberlain's Barn Quarry
BRYAN'S LOOP
Abrahams Farm
VANDYKE JUNCTION (Co-op Loop)
GRAND UNION CANAL
CLIPSTONE BROOK
SWING SWANG BRIDGE
LINSLADE TUNNEL
LEIGHTON BUZZARD
LINSLADE
VANDYKE ROAD
HOCKLIFFE ROAD A4012
HOCKLIFFE
Leedon Farm
LEEDON LOOP
Clay Pit
B4032
BUCKINGHAM
Marley Roof Tiles
MARLEY'S BANK
STANBRIDGE ROAD LOOP
EGGINGTON
LEIGHTON BUZZARD STATION
ALL SAINT'S CHURCH
H G Brown Pit
CONCRETE WORKS
STANBRIDGE ROAD
Jennings Pit
Gregory Harris Pit
PAGE'S PARK
GROVEBURY
RED BARN LOOP
Pratt's Pit
AYLESBURY A418
Rackley Hill Pit
WHARF
Rails still in situ (1997)
Tile works
George Garside's Pits
Firbanks Pit
Spinney Pool
LEIGHTON-LINSLADE BY PASS
DUNSTABLE
A4146
HEMEL HEMPSTEAD
Grovebury Pit
RIVER OUZEL
EUSTON - LONDON
0
½ mile
1 mile

Acknowledgements

In the course of explaining some of the early background to the Leighton Buzzard Light Railway I have read *The Leighton Buzzard Light Railway* by Sydney Leleux (Oakwood Press, 1969). A second enlarged edition was published in 1996. This book provides a much fuller and more comprehensive description of the sand quarry railways in Leighton Buzzard and their operations. As such the book forms a useful companion to the photographs in *Narrow Gauge Tracks in the Sand*.

I also wish to thank the following for their assistance in providing archival information:

Sydney Leleux	Alan Keef
Chris Daniels	Alf Fisher
Peter Arnold	William Shelford
David White	Tony Tomkins
Bob Blake	Tom Lawson

My gratitude also goes to the many members of the Leighton Buzzard Narrow Gauge Railway Society for their support over many years, especially William Shelford the society's archivist. Credit must also go to the photographers particularly Kevin Lane, who has provocatively captured the final years of the LBLR operations.

I must also express my thanks to David Barrow for the preparation of the maps which appear in this book.

Finally much praise must go to Chris Daniels for his encouragement and help over a great period of time, for expert advice, and for proof-reading *Narrow Gauge Tracks in the Sand*.

Population Growth of Leighton Buzzard

Year	*No. of People*
1086	700
1671	1,276
1717	1,634
1801	2,166
1811	2,395
1821	3,119
1831	3,737
1841	4,848
1851	5,774
1861	5,841
1871	7,041
1881	7,715
1891	8,686
1901	8,488
1911	9,044
1921	9,170
1931	9,463
1939	11,043
1951	12,295
1961	15,884
1971	20,347
1981	29,772
1991	31,855

A view of Leighton Buzzard High Street taken from a Valentine's Series picture postcard.

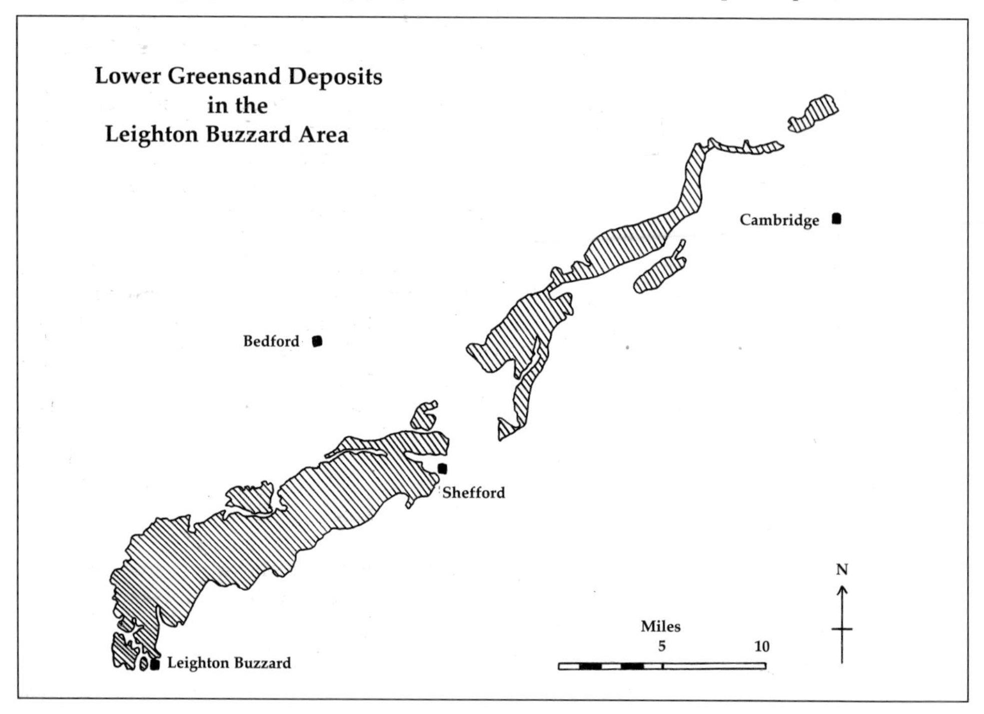

Sand Town

During the past 200 years the town of Leighton Buzzard in South Bedfordshire has relied for much of its growth and prosperity on the mining of its natural resource - sand. From small scratchings the industry developed until it played a major role in the affairs of the local community. As well as producing sand, many people were involved with its transportation and subsequent manufacturing use. Today, sand no longer has the same influence in the district that it once did, with many of the subsidiary industries, born out of the sand trade, now playing an equally important role in their own right.

In recent times many new and different companies have moved into the area. The town has become part of the commuter belt for London-based workers, many of whom could not even begin to appreciate the significance sand once played in the lives of the local population, not so long ago.

The lower greensand found in the terrain around Leighton Buzzard was laid down as marine deposits in the lower cretaceous era. The outcrop crosses the region from a south-westerly direction, several miles wide stretching towards the north-east in the direction of Cambridge. Over 70 grades of sand have been found in beds buried beneath the surface, these range in colouration from white to black, geologically however, silver or silica sand is the substance most in demand. Due to its special mechanical and chemical characteristics silica sand unearthed at Leighton Buzzard is economically important as a raw material for industrial purposes. For instance it forms the basic ingredient in glass making, whether it be for the humble milk bottle or modern fibre optic cable. The sand is ideally suited for ceramics, plastics and also for water treatment processes.

Another major application for sand acquired from the Leighton Buzzard quarries is its consumption in foundries where resin coated sand mouldings are used in the casting of precision machinery. So many objects manufactured this way affect our daily lives, for example the motor car. At one stage Ford's in Dagenham were supplied with 320 tons of sand every day from standard gauge wagons leaving local exchange sidings. In Leighton Buzzard itself brick, tile and concrete plants took thousands of tons of sand each year direct from the pits. Because of its exceptionally high quality, the sand found in Leighton Buzzard is used as an international standard and has been exported throughout the world, even to the Sahara Desert.

The sand today is mainly quarried by two companies: Joseph Arnold & Sons Ltd (Arnold White Group PLC, 1993), this business was sold to Hepworth Minerals & Chemicals in July 1995. The second company, George Garside (Sand) Ltd was taken over by English China Clay in November 1978 since June 1994 the company has been owned by Camas Aggregates Ltd.

Other companies in the locality include ARC's Buckland Sand & Silica, Hall Aggregates Ltd and LB Silica Sand Ltd.

Removing the Clay

The sand is taken from pits mainly to the south-east and north sides of Leighton Buzzard. It is found beneath a layer of clay and iron sandstone of varying depths, some fairly shallow.

A Leighton Buzzard sand quarry in 1948. The scene is typical of the time, with clay overburden being removed. Men with ladders stand halfway up the exposed face shovelling sand down to the screening plant. A newly-delivered locomotive is ready to take the sand away on the rickety narrow gauge railway. *Chris Daniels Collection*

Removal of Overburden *c.* 1910. The workers include: second left, Arthur Woolhead; third left, Albert Woolhead; right, Tom Hedges. The Foreman in the background was known as 'Stand Up' because he used to stand up all day to keep an eye on output. Chalk tally marks can just be seen on the right-hand skip showing the number filled so far that day by the gang.

Vera & Arthur Shales

A working quarry *c.* 1920, showing clay strata and the sand face. *Joseph Arnold & Sons Ltd*

A barrow run at Twenty One Acre Quarry in 1930. The overburden is tipped into a worked out section of the pit as the 22 ft deep sand face expands. *Arnold White PLC*

Nine Acre Quarry (formerly Chance's Quarry) in 1940. Clay overburden is being removed by a steam excavator and skips. Note the three sand benches are just the height of the ladders being used. *Joseph Arnold & Sons Ltd*

Spoil being removed by a 10RB excavator with driver Jack Kimble at the controls. Albert Stanley Webb, known as Stan to his friends was also an excavator driver with Arnold's. Stan used to leave home to go to work by bicycle each day at 4.30 am to arrive at 5 am. He then began the long task of building up steam for the excavator used for 'topping' i.e. removing overburden. He used to wear a red and white neckerchief which was also useful for wrapping his sandwiches in.

Jeff Johnson

An excavator and workers at rest beside the clay face. *Arthur Webb Collection*

Horse-powered 'trains' of six skips at the sand face *c.* 1920. It was easier to throw sand down into the skips from the ledge above.

Joseph Arnold & Sons Ltd

The clay was used extensively in the manufacture of bricks.* The sandstone element, which often required blasting to break and dislodge, was used in huge quantities for building up the sides of the local A5 road (Watling Street) in the days of the stage coach. It also had a limited use as a building stone, St Andrew's Church, unfortunately demolished in 1970, and Stonehenge Works being prime examples.

In the early days, the clay overburden was removed by a gang of four men who carved a 20 ft-wide horizontal channel into the sand, just under the solid strata of clay. The whole working face was supported by three columns of sand which were left intact. When everything was prepared, the pillars were chopped away causing huge banks of clay to come crashing down. The diggers carrying out this exercise had to run like mad to escape being crushed. Often there were casualties, some of which were fatal. The whole procedure was known as 'topping'. It was back-breaking labour but the men were fit and were used to long hard days of spadework, toiling in all weathers. Once the operation was over the spoil was removed in wheelbarrows to a part of the pit that had been worked out.

In some cases it was necessary to build trestle bridges spanning the quarry. These barrow runs made life much easier and enabled the clay to be transported to the tipping area without being dragged wearily through the sand. On other occasions in order to lengthen and widen the working face a ledge was dug beside the clay on top of the exposed sand. A section of track was laid on this ridge and the overburden was then loaded into rail-mounted wagons. These skips could then be pushed one by one, or sometimes pulled behind a horse, to the exhausted portion of the quarry so that spoil could be disposed of. Later, steam driven excavators were introduced, the increased development causing all the clay to be transported by rail. Today the overburden is removed by gigantic bulldozers and scrapers taking just a few days to expose thousands of tons of sand.

Excavating the Sand

In the beginning, sand excavation in Leighton Buzzard, started with numerous small scratchings. However around 1790 these began to develop more strongly and trade in sand expanded rapidly.

Arthur Shales, who worked for Arnold's for over 50 years describes how the sand was obtained in the early days.

> The sand was dug by men, or 'dobbers', as we were known working on piece rates. Higher wages were paid according to the grade of material being loaded in to the wagons. Excavating the best quality sand meant more money could be earned. The normal practice was to dislodge the sand by climbing ladders stretching high up the side of the sand cliffs. At the top we would gouge out a tiny ledge just wide enough to stand on. From this precarious position the sand was scooped down over the edge of the working face ready to shovel up into wagons. You had to be very cautious in case the

* Bedfordshire is famous for its bricks, although manufacture was not centred on Leighton Buzzard there were nevertheless a large number of brickmakers in the town using the Gault blue clay obtained from the quarries. The principal sites were located at Grovebury Farm, Hockliffe Road, Plantation Road, Row Riddy Stone, Stanbridge Road and Vandyke Road.

A train ready to be hauled out of the quarry *c.* 1920. The rails would be repositioned closer to the face as the ledge was eaten away.
Joseph Arnold & Sons Ltd

sand gave way beneath your feet. Luckily the sand was soft if you did happen to slip over the edge. As a short cut we developed a method of cutting horizontal grooves into the base of the sand face so that the whole working section would slide down. When the sand started to slip we did not turn round and run as we did in the case of the clay landslides but instead we faced the avalanche and dived to lay flat on top of the sand as it raced toward us. It was dangerous, but at least we were not buried face down by the sand overtaking us from behind. Whilst working we tied string round the bottom of our trouser legs so the sand did not get into our boots. The sand was then loaded into horse-drawn wagons or directly into carts and taken away.

Because the sand was easy to shovel into the wagons by hand men continued to carry out this work for many years after mechanical methods were available. Between 24 and 30 wagons were loaded per man each day. At Double Arches a gang of 13 men was employed at the face.

In the 1930s the first excavators appeared in the pits to help load the sand into wagons. Until drivers got used to dropping the sand in the right position a pole was often stuck upright marking the far corner of the skip to give them guidance. Another device designed to ensure that sand was not spilled and wasted in between the skips was an inverted 'V' shaped metal template, this was placed on top of the wagons over the couplings, as the sand was tipped it was diverted into the skips. Despite the arrival of mechanical aids, hand loading continued and did not cease in the Arnold's quarries until the mid-1960s. POWs captured in World War II extended manual labour in the Garside pits to 1945, by which time Ruston Bucyrus face shovels and draglines replaced much of the donkey work. Looking into the quarries today excavators, face shovels and draglines can still be seen at work amongst the more modern equipment.

To remove the impurities the sand was first sifted by throwing it through a sieve placed over the wagon or cart being loaded. The screen was positioned at an angle allowing the unwanted material to cascade down and out whilst the sorted sand fell through the mesh.

Later, when various grades of sand were required for different industries, other ways and means had to be found to sieve the sand into the required grain sizes.

Initially two main forms of plant were installed, the first type was the 'Shaker' consisting of a vibrating riddle in which the sand dropped through ½ in. holes. This machine was ideal for the purpose of screening building sand. Other sands had to be much finer, especially for use in foundries; in this case a washing procedure was introduced. It was particularly important during World War I when so much of this grade of sand was needed for the manufacture of armaments.

This method developed into the 'Niagara', a double decked device for washing sand whereby a steady stream of water, initially running over a vibrating screen of ½ in. mesh, separated the larger materials. The remainder dropped down to the lower ⅛ in. screen which was made of piano wires. The procedure produced the best results and increased tonnage.

A further filtration process got rid of the unwanted particles of silt, pumping it away to merge with sediment previously disposed of elsewhere in the exhausted workings of the quarry.

Sand being screened at Nine Acre Quarry (formerly Chance's Pit) in 1940. *Joseph Arnold & Sons Ltd*

Barrel washers comprised of revolving cylinders with gaps of gradually increasing degrees soon replaced the 'Niagara'. The apparatus scooped up piles of sand in buckets fixed to a conveyor belt then fed it into a long, slowly rotating drum. Depending on its coarseness the sand eventually descended down chutes into wagons stationed on sidings below ready to be hauled away.

Some of the machinery used in the quarries was made locally by Shepherd Bros whose premises were situated in Ashwell Street near St Andrew's Church in Leighton Buzzard.

Heading towards the collection point *c.* 1920s. *Arnold White PLC*

Sand excavation in progress. Note the use of the skip height platform for easier loading.
Joseph Arnold & Sons Ltd

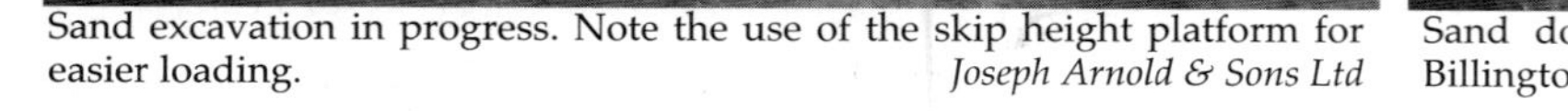

Sand dobbers Reeves and Lee hard at work at Arnold's washery in Billington Road *c.* 1925.
Tom Lawson Collection

Double Arches dobbers, Tom Hedges is second on the left. *Arthur Webb Collection*

Sand dobbers taking a break, left to right: unknown; standing, Alvin Hedges; sitting, Mr Capp; lying, Len Wallace; standing, Ted Brantom, Shady Turner and Fred Wells who was known as 'Pigeon'. *Jack Brantom Collection*

A fine example of a sand screen built by local manufacturer Shepherd Bros for a Leighton Buzzard quarry. Note St Andrew's Church in the background. *Chris Daniels Collection*

Sand washing in the quarry, probably Double Arches, *c.* 1920. *Colin Holmes Collection*

The washing and screening plant at Double Arches in 1940.

Arnold White PLC

Above: Barrow runs at Firbank Pit. In the background the Leighton Buzzard to Dunstable branch of the LNWR and the gas works can be seen. On the siding in the foreground sand is being loaded into standard gauge wagons.
Tom Lawson Collection

Right: Joseph Firbank, railway contractor 1819-1886. *Author's Collection*

Soon brickmakers and builders' merchants wanted more and more sand as towns in the neighbourhood began to extend their boundaries, individual sand pit owners prospered. This was the age when the sand carter came into existence; these olden days kings of the road were very independent characters and had a mischievous reputation to live up to as they plied their trade around the district.

Horses and carts were taken right up to the quarry face to be loaded, often sleeper roads had to be put down to stop the wheels from sinking and getting stuck; this applied especially in wet conditions when parts of the quarry often turned to quicksand. In some pits tramways were laid, this enabled the sand to be moved by horse-drawn wagons and tipped by the road for collection.

At this time the sand carter probably travelled no more than a 30 miles radius of Leighton Buzzard, but as the years went by business gradually grew from a purely local trade into a national activity. Leighton Buzzard sand was transported to ever increasing distances as demand for the mineral spread further afield. Transportation was helped in 1800 with the opening of the Grand Junction Canal (Grand Union Canal from 1929) which meant it was even easier to convey the sand all over the country, especially to new markets in the Midlands and the North.

In these days huge quantities of sand was loaded into narrow boats destined for the short journey down to London. Here it was needed for construction work during the Regency period, when much of the West End of the capital was built. Shipments of sand were also sent by the inland waterways to the heart of the British manufacturing industry in Birmingham. Regular trips went to Messrs Chance's Glass Works in Wolverhampton and Smethwick. The company manufactured fine quality glassware including lenses for many of Britain's coastal lighthouses. The journey took five days with up to 90 tons of sand being carried in three narrow boats drawn by horses. Messrs Chance's had their own pit beside Miletree Road. In 1878 thirty of their horses and carts alone were daily ferrying sand to the canalside wharves.

Another boost to the sand trade occurred in 1838 when the London and Birmingham Railway [London & North Western Railway (LNWR) in 1846] decided to build its railway through Leighton Buzzard. After much hostility by influential people in the town the railway company eventually constructed the line and a station a short distance away in the village of Linslade. The London and Birmingham Railway started on the outskirts of London in a small village named Euston and proceeded northwards to Birmingham with intervening stations being built along the way.

In this fast moving age a contractor named Joseph Firbank had undertaken the task of adding a third running line on the LNWR route from Willesden to Tring, a distance of 26 miles. The contract commenced in 1857 and was completed in 1859. Further north, sidings were laid at Wolverton. Between 1860 and 1862 Firbank was busy building the Bedford to Cambridge branch.

Ten years later found him returning to the metropolis again , this time he was responsible for the Swiss Cottage to Harrow Extension (1878-1880). To help facilitate the construction work which consisted of numerous new stations along the routes, and associated bridges, embankments, *et al*, Joseph Firbank decided that it would be better to draw on his own source of sand.

Consequently he opened his own quarry in Leighton Buzzard, to provide all

Joseph Arnold 1841-1911. *Arnold White PLC*

the sand that he wanted, whilst the contracts were in hand. Firbank's Pit was situated on the southern side of Union Street (later Grovebury Road) and was the first major quarry to be excavated in the town.

The Leighton Buzzard to Dunstable branch, opened in 1848, passed just a few feet away from Firbank's Pit. It certainly seems to have been an ideal location as subsequently a new centre for sand distribution, with sidings and tipping docks, was based at Grovebury. Sand was transported to the new facilities for onward shipment nationwide.

The carters of Leighton Buzzard were now busier than ever taking sand either to the railway sidings or to the canal wharves. What could possibly threaten this prosperous trade? It was the coming of the narrow gauge railway that eventually brought their demise. A long and colourful obituary to the sand carter was published in the 2nd December, 1919 edition of the *Leighton Buzzard Observer* to mark his demise.

Joseph Arnold & Sons Ltd

It was in the 1850s that a local family named Arnold who were previously carpenters by trade, changed their profession to builders' merchants and finally to sand pit owners.

It might be a coincidence but long before these changes took place there is a record of one Latham Arnold, a tobacconist from London, owning Sandpit Cottage and two sandpits along Miletree Road from 1734 until 1759. One of these pits is obviously Mile Tree Road Sand Mine, later Twenty One Acre Quarry and was the spot where the existence of silver sand was first discovered.

We do not know whether Latham Arnold was a distant relation of the Arnold family that really began the sand industry in Leighton Buzzard 100 years later. The company that bears the Arnold name today was started by John Arnold around 1860 when he was in his early forties. John lived at Heath and Reach, about two miles north of Leighton Buzzard, where he opened Stone Hill Lane Pit producing high quality building sand. Although strong the business was still fairly small with just one pit providing all the sand for which customers could be found. Much of this sand was sent by rail to London where his eldest son Joseph, who was living in Camden Town, trading as a builders' merchant, secured orders for it.

Amongst the major customers Arnold's dealt with was Joseph Firbank, supplying sand to many of his works, in particular to the Midland Railway's St Pancras Goods Depot in Somers Town which was enlarged in 1884. The scheme required 3,000 houses to be demolished in Agar Town and 500 dwellings in Somers Town. One of the first works taken in hand was a magnificent wall, ¾ mile in length, 30 ft high and 3 ft thick. This surrounded the entire site. Eight million bricks were used. Judging from the business that Arnold's obtained it would appear that Joseph Firbank had established a good, friendly, trading relationship with the emerging new sand quarry owners, and might have been influential in other ways.

When John Arnold died in 1880 he left his business to his three sons, Joseph, John Alfred, who was a missionary, and George. For a short period the

Ernest Arnold (*right*) at a building trades exhibition in 1901 with George Balchin (*left*). *Arnold White PLC*

JOSEPH ARNOLD'S

Special Silicate Sands!

THE LEADING TRADE ARTICLE!

Admitted and universally recognized by all Practical Judges the Best Sand in the Market, being always reliable!

(Established 40 Years).

PLASTERING TESTS with J. ARNOLD's Sands are here shown, guaged with Portland Cement, also Keen's, Seraptite, Parian and other Patent Cements, also Lime and Hair Mortar, in the usual proportion of composite mixing. (Messrs. Bazley White's and Francis & Co.'s Portland Cements have been used in connexion herewith, and the results are equally convincing against the possibility of anything approaching to a Failure? but the Reverse!

My Silicate Sand is in three grades: Coarse, for 1st and 2nd coat, Medium or Fine, for finishing coat—requires no washing, screening or preparation before using.

Prices are low and less than Thames prepared sand washed and screened, and without that trouble—therefore it must be cheapest and by far the safest.

Subjoined are some important works by whom this sand has been used and given the greatest satisfaction:

Westminster Cathedral.
London United Tramway Co.'s Power House.
Strand Electric Co.'s do. do.
Blackwall Tunnel Works.
Hackney Baths.
St. Pancras Baths.
Islington Electric Station.
Central London Railway.
Great Central Railway.
L. & N. W. Ry. (Crewe Extension Works).

Kilsby Tunnel Works.
Midland Ry. (widening Kentish Town).
Midland Ry. (Somers Town do.)
East London Water Works (for Filtration).
New River Co. ,,
Grand Junction ,,
Birmingham Corporation ,,
Northampton do. ,,
Worcester do. ,,
Leicester do. ,,
and other Provincial Water Companies.

Prices can be had on application for delivery to any part of the Metropolitan area. Orders booked here and sent direct to pits for immediate despatch.

STAND NO. 124, ROW F, *or to* 32, ST. PAUL'S RD., CAMDEN TOWN, LONDON, N.W.

Building Trades' Exhibition, Agricultural Hall, Islington, N., April 17 to 27, 1901.

Telegrams: "SANDBAGS, LONDON." **Telephone: 334 Kings Cross.**

Advertising *c.* 1901 detailing many works built with Arnold's sands.

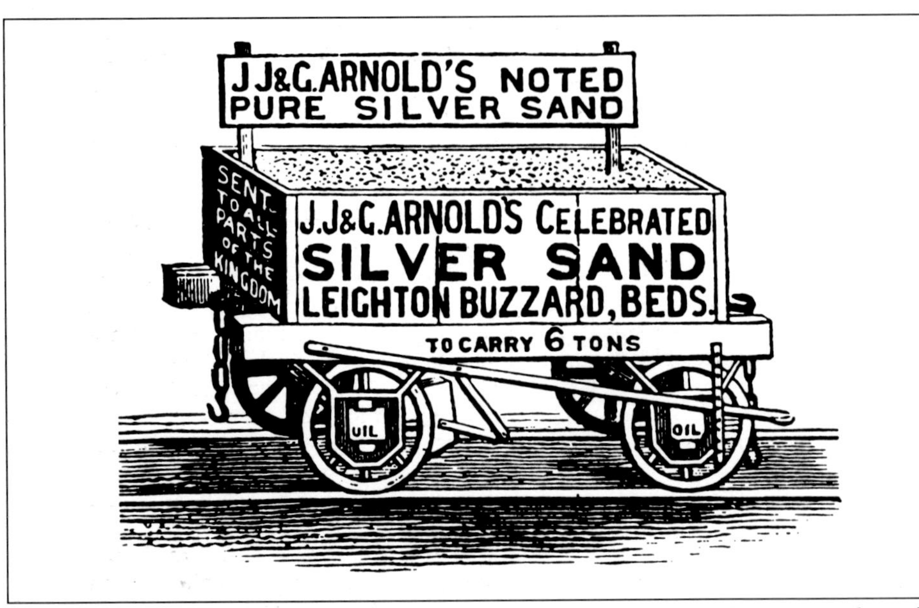

Letter head and advertising feature which was especially used on envelope-type packets of matches *c.* 1875. J.J. & G. is thought to stand for John, Joseph and George. George soon left the business to go his own way. *Joseph Arnold & Sons Ltd*

Spinney Pool Quarry *c.* 1880 which later became a popular swimming pool (1921). This postcard was issued depicting the delights of Leighton Buzzard. Note the skips on the right of the picture!

partnership continued to manage affairs but but it was not long before Joseph took complete control of the whole enterprise and made the business his own. Letter headings announcing 'Joseph Arnold' appeared 10 years later, although George was still not happy with the situation even then.

From the very beginning Joseph was determined to make a success of the business. He possessed tremendous energy and was a man of more than ordinary foresight and commercial ability.

As soon as practicable a London office was established at 32, St Pauls Road (now Agar Road) where he could promote the unique qualities of Leighton Buzzard sand and attract orders. Additional premises were obtained nearby at 1a, Elm Road which was situated next to the goods depot at Euston station. This property included stables and made it possible for him to oversee the onward conveyance of his sand. It might also have been stockpiled here ready to supply various important customers in and around the capital. An office was also set up at 24, Market Square, Leighton Buzzard for local enquiries.

Very soon it appears the quest for extra business began to pay dividends with Government orders to supply sand for water and sewage filtration works. As a result of this he was able to declare that he was a 'Contractor to Her Majesty's Government'.

The welcome work brought with it problems to solve, these were cured by the purchase of additional quarries in Leighton Buzzard which enabled Joseph Arnold to supply the special grades of sand needed for different types of work. Mile Tree Sand Mine was bought, to become known as Twenty One Acre Quarry, also Chance's Pit which was later named Nine Acre Quarry. Rackley Hill Pit to the west of Grovebury level crossing was also purchased around this time and proved ideal for building sand, from which the Blackwall Tunnel and Hackney Public Baths were built in 1897.

As well as adjoining the LNWR sidings Rackley Hill Pit was also connected by 2 ft gauge railway (*c.* 1895) to the Grand Junction Canal. To achieve this Joseph Arnold constructed a bridge over the River Ouzel at a cost of £1,000 and constructed a canalside wharf enabling his sand to be tipped directly into narrow boats moored beside the quay.

Joseph Arnold's masterful salesmanship, especially to London builders, was extremely forthcoming as witnessed by an impressive list of works for which he provided the sand. This list was produced in an advertisement printed for the Building Trade Exhibition in 1901.

By the turn of the 19th century the special qualities of Leighton Buzzard sand were well recognised and new markets were opening throughout the country. The extraordinary increase in turnover was put back in to the business and soon Joseph Arnold was buying even more quarries, together with surrounding land, which he hoped would safeguard all his foreseeable requirements.

Joseph was not one to sit still, first buying Spinney Pool which became the home of the Leighton Buzzard Swimming Club (in 1921), this like Pratt's Pit was situated in Billington Road.

As demand for sand continued unabated Joseph Arnold turned his attention to the north of Leighton Buzzard for new supplies purchasing land that was to become Chamberlain's Barn Quarry in 1912 and Double Arches Quarry in 1916. Earlier he

Arnold's had seven narrow boats for conveying their sand. This photograph shows *John* and *Joseph* being towed empty by horse at Berkhamsted.

British Waterways Archives, Gloucester

opened a quarry at Flitwick, nine miles north-east of Leighton Buzzard, in 1902.

With ever increasing trade, ways of saving on transport costs were investigated. This resulted in Arnold's investing in their own fleet of horse-drawn narrow boats which were named *Albert Joseph, Caroline Elizabeth, John, Joseph, Thomas, Felix* and *Albert*. They also later commisioned 30 standard gauge railway wagons which were signwritten and painted in red oxide livery.

Joseph Arnold was the 'father' of the sand trade in Leighton Buzzard his fame as a sand merchant was well known. By the time of his death in 1911, through sheer dynamism, he had laid the foundations of a successful industry that was to prove a worthwhile legacy for future generations.

Two years before he died Joseph passed the business to his sons Albert and Ernest. They had already been involved with the running of the company for many years and had even owned their own sand quarry at Stone, near Aylesbury.

Albert and Ernest were to be involved in some major operational changes in their lifetimes, mostly in regard to the transportation of sand. However, as far as the quarries were concerned they soon started to rationalise and improve matters along different lines. Firstly the brothers built a new depot in Union Street (Grovebury Road) on a site formerly known as Jennings Pit. The depot provided washing and grading facilities for most of Arnold's output that could not be handled within the quarries. The plant was not rail connected to the LNWR sidings so the continued movement of sand was extremely troublesome, horses and carts being used as well as steam wagons. This problem was later solved by the building of a new washing plant with better facilities in the northern corner of Gregory Harris' old pit, situated beside Billington Road, opposite Page's Park. At this location a rail-mounted tipping dock enabled sand to be loaded directly into standard gauge wagons shunted into Grovebury Sidings. In this period of rationalisation Rackley Hill Quarry was sold.

In 1918 the name of the business was changed to Joseph Arnold & Sons (this became a Limited Company in 1937). Also in 1918 a new office was opened at 124, Tottenham Court Road, in London, to replace the St Pauls Road address.

In 1921 Albert and Ernest were amongst the founders of the Leighton Buzzard Glass Works built beside Billington Road; they hoped to improve the market for glass bottles. However, the venture was never successful and the factory was sold seven years later. The last of the canal fleet was also sold in 1923.

By now Double Arches Quarry had become one of the largest in the UK with a working face 600 yards long and 30 ft in height.

Albert and Ernest's major achievement though was the formation of the Leighton Buzzard Light Railway in 1919. Upon Albert's death in 1939 Ernest continued to run the company until he died in 1949. It was during this period that many new industries, all of which required sand were built beside the light railway line. Brick companies, tile factories and cement works took a considerable portion of the sand produced in the quarries via the 2 ft gauge track and its branches.

As Albert's marriage had produced four daughters it was Ernest's sons, Joseph Ernest and Frederick, who continued to manage the company from 1950. The daughters, though, had half-ownership held in trust for them for life, this being administered by two trustees.

After World War II the business carried on as before with thousands of tons

Arnold's depot in Union Street (now Grovebury Road) *c.* 1930s. Those identified in the photograph are Joseph Ernest Arnold in the foreground with Mr Saunders just behind him. Mr Toms stands on the gantry above them.

Joseph Arnold & Sons Ltd

Arnold's Billington Road washery *c.* 1930s with equipment transferred from Union Street depot. *Joseph Arnold & Sons Ltd*

Albert Arnold 1875-1939.

Ernest Arnold 1879-1949.

Joseph Ernest Arnold, born 1907.

Frederick Arnold 1910-1991

(All) Arnold White PLC

of sand being carried along the light railway to the standard gauge sidings. However, restrictions on road transport were gradually eased and the quantity of sand dispatched by rail began its steady decline.

In 1955 British Railways suffered a national strike as a result of which many customers turned to road transport, never to return to the railways. This state of affairs resulted in customers arranging to collect sand by lorry themselves as well as having deliveries made to them by Arnold's haulage contractors, Biggs. To cope with the change of circumstances road weighbridges had to be installed in the quarries.

Despite this threat New Trees Quarry was opened in 1964 at Shenley Hill Road. It was connected to the light railway by a ½ mile-long branch line leading from Chamberlain's Barn Quarry. The omens were bad, the railway being destined to exist for only six years before being dismantled in favour of road transport.

In 1967 the Tottenham Court Road office was closed and administration transferred to Billington Road in Leighton Buzzard. It was in this year that negotiations with what was to become the Leighton Buzzard Narrow Gauge Railway Society commenced for use of the light railway track. Before the last remnants of the Dunstable-Leighton Buzzard branch was closed in December 1969 the preservation group had agreed with Joseph E. to take responsibility for a section of the line to Vandyke Road. This was later extended as use of the line ceased. When both Joseph E. and Frederick retired as Managing Directors of the company in 1980 it was left to Joseph's son, Peter Arnold, to run the business; he owned a quarter of the shares.

With Peter in control he commenced on a programme of modernisation which saw many changes. A complete replacement of the plant at Double Arches was instigated and other machinery relocated. Much of the equipment installed in the quarries years ago needed renewing. Sand was still being produced for building, brickmaking, tilemaking, plastering, water filtration, foundry work, horticulture and leisure markets, but somehow the industry had to be revitalised and new markets found. In the late 1980s the company took a new direction through the influence of Albert Arnold's four daughters' half-share ownership of the business.

One of the girls, Marjorie, married a man named Morris White who was the owner of a large company of Luton-based builders called Robinson & White, formed in 1920. Before this, however, the White side of the business went back for another 200 years. With the White family representatives on the Board, Peter Arnold continued with his quest of finding a new stratagy to make the quarries more commercial again.

When Frederick Arnold transferred his shares to Robinson & White before he died in 1991 the new company took majority control. A year later Peter Arnold decided to relinquish his holding in favour of Robinson & White, which lead to the formation of a new company entitled the Arnold White Group PLC, in 1992.

Following the collapse into receivership of the construction side of the Arnold White Group in 1994 the Arnold sand business was sold, in 1995, to Hepworth Minerals & Chemicals (formerly British Industrial Sands).

John Arnold	1816-1880	Joseph Ernest Arnold	1907-
Joseph Arnold	1841-1911	Frederick Arnold	1910-1991
Albert Arnold	1875-1939	Peter Arnold	1945-
Ernest Arnold	1879-1949		

George Garside 1848-1926.
George Garside (Sand) Ltd

Hugh Delafield 1891-1957.
George Garside (Sand) Ltd

George Garside (Sand) Ltd

Adjacent to the Arnold's depot in Billington Road another sand company had previously set up their own washing and screening plant, together with loading docks giving them access to the Grovebury Road Sidings. The quarry owner was George Garside who was destined to become the second biggest sand merchant in Leighton Buzzard.

George Garside began trading in sand around 1890, before this date he was involved in brick making and the building business.* Instead of dealing with suppliers he thought it beneficial to have his own source of sand. An office was set up at 28, Lake Street. An old quarry in Billington Road was his first venture but it was soon exhausted so he used part of the pit to establish his firm's washery. Two smaller pits were then opened near the old Firbank Quarry in Grovebury Road.

To expand even further he purchased from Arnold's, Rackley Hill Quarry which gradually became flooded as it went deeper; by now he had moved his headquarters to the White House, a lovely Italianate building. Having no children George Garside was assisted by his nephew Hugh Delafield, this partnership was interrupted briefly by World War I when Hugh became a soldier.

After the conflict a new quarry was opened in the water meadows beyond Grovebury Farm, half a mile away from the other workings, this was called Grovebury Pit. This quarry, from its inception in 1926 lay below the water table and so is naturally flooded; here the sand is removed by a suction dredger which floats on the surface of the resulting lake.

In the same year Munday's Hill was developed, here pure white sand could be found. Sadly, George Garside did not live to see this expand for he died in October at the age of 78 leaving the business to be managed by Hugh Delafield on behalf of his widow until she died in 1931. Mrs Garside had always enjoyed the tradition of travelling down to Paddington Basin on one of the company's own fleet of narrow boats to hand out oranges to the boat children over the Easter Festivals. The narrow boats were named, *Forget Me Not, Dorothy, Nancy, Nellie, Rose, Duke, Evelyn, Linney, Hugh, Dauntless* and *Vera*.

Hugh Delafield's first duty was the abstraction of sand from two further quarries located at the far end of the Leighton Buzzard Light Railway system. Rail transportation enabled him to develop Long Stretch which started in about 1930 and was to last for 20 years before being abandoned. Nearby Churchways, located at a lower level, opened in the same period, producing yellow sand. Part of the quarry became flooded and had to be excavated by a dredger, this pumped sand and water to land based screens. This operation continued until 1960 when it was decided to expand the workings above the water table.

Hugh Delafield controlled the company until 1957 when the firm passed to his two sons, J.G. & W.H. Delafield, who formed the business into a limited company in 1960. Immediately they set about the establishment of a large new washing and drying plant at Eastern Way, near to Munday's Hill Quarry, this proved its worth a few years later.

English China Clays, who took over the company in November 1978, continued the modernisation programme. Following a demerger in 1994, the company, which still trades under the name of George Garside (Sand) Ltd, is now owned by Camas Aggregates Ltd.

* In this connection he will be remembered for many new estates in Leighton Buzzard and Linslade including those built around George Street which was named after him. Hockliffe Street Baptist Church was also one of his achievements.

A regular run for George Garside's narrow boats was to Paddington Basin. *Linney* and *Nellie* are seen here at Batchworth Lock, near Rickmansworth.

Railway & Canal Historical Society

GEORGE GARSIDE,
Building and Silver
Sand
Pit Owner,
LEIGHTON BUZZARD.
Sand of all kinds and for all purposes
in connection with Building, Water
— Filtration, Horticultural Work, etc. —
— —Washed Sand a Speciality.— —
Standard Sand for Cement Testing
—————a Speciality.—— ———
Private Wharves on Rail and
Canal at Leighton Buzzard,
nearly 500 acres in extent for
—————working.—————
The Only Address:—
GEORGE GARSIDE,
Leighton Buzzard. -

A view of the level crossing at Billington Road on the Leighton Buzzard to Dunstable branch of the LNWR in 1917. The state of the roads caused by the sand traffic was absolutely deplorable.

County Record Office, Bedford

One of Arnold's 'Clayton' steam wagons. Bernard Farr, age 15, is seen second from the left.

Author's Collection

Roads

Prior to World War I sand was shifted from the pits by horse and cart, resulting in appalling damage to the dirt roads in and around Leighton Buzzard. In the winter months these tracks were often impassable due to mud, which was literally knee deep. The route to the railway sidings and canal went through the centre of Leighton Buzzard, Lake Street in particular being atrocious to traverse, being choked with potholes and deep ruts. The major roads were eventually tarmacadamed. However, this improvement only brought further trouble when steam wagons were introduced for haulage.

At one time Joseph Arnold had a fleet of 23 steam wagons, a regular run was to Aylesbury and back. The roads were so bad in the winter months that a steam wagon was often the only way to get from A to B. The steam wagons offered some advantages, but not to the already ravaged roads which took a fearful punishment. As compensation vast sums of money had to be paid to local government by the sand companies in retribution for all the damage caused. This reduced their profits considerably. It was a major handicap that had to be overcome as the expense had to be passed on and included in customers' charges. Another factor which did not improve the situation was competition in the form of cheap imported sand, especially from Belgium.

This sand was used as ballast in vessels returning from the continent and, quite literally, dumped in this country. It made little sense for merchants in the Midlands and North of England to buy sand all the way from Leighton Buzzard when all they had to do was arrange to collect it from their local docks at far less cost.

To compete against this opposition the sand companies had to cut their overheads; it was a serious problem, something had to be done.

A.C. Biggs' lorry fleet with driver Frank Oakley centre. *Frank Oakley Collection*

Below left: A 1918, 50 cwt. Hallgate lorry, chain drive, gate change with solid tyres driven by Ted Brantom in 1924. Jack Brantom recalls,

The Hallgate was a World War I lorry, and had the army paint underneath its 'civvy' green, it was my father's pride and joy. The first fun I recall was when Stockgrove mansion was being built. He went up with a load of building sand until an excavation in the road stopped his progress. The building workers would be laid off if they did not get their sand. At this point Father took off into the woods (fully loaded and with solid tyres!), he told me afterwards, 'I knew if I could find a way through the trees without stopping I would make it', and this he did, delivering the sand and returning following his own wheeltracks. The other great excitement was when the lorry 'spat back' once too often down Church Hill and caught fire. He pulled up at the 'Star' in Heath Road. The petrol pipe had melted under the bonnet and petrol was running out onto the road and down the gutter burning as it went. Father reached up under the side of the body and managed to turn off the petrol, whilst Wally Evans, who happened to be passing, nipped up onto the back of the lorry and shovelled sand onto the road whilst dad shovelled it into the engine compartment and eventually got control. She looked a sorry state after this and was declared scrap, but Dad set to work on her, cadging, improvising and restoring engine and bodywork. After working night and day, and with a quick repaint she was back on the road in three weeks. His enthusiasm and confidence were not shared by the powers that be, and it was decided to swap it for a more modern vehicle from London. The day arrived, 1½ cwt. of tools and equipment were loaded onto the old girl to give him every chance of getting her there in one piece. She never missed a beat. Holding her straight in the London traffic made his arms ache (there was a third of a turn play in the steering). The new (second-hand) vehicle was started up and run round the block; all seemed well so all the tackle was transferred and then away. A few miles up the road she conked out. All the normal checks were done, nothing much appeared wrong, he had a cup of tea swung the crank and off she went. A few more miles up the road she stopped again, this was to continue all the way to Leighton Buzzard, in the course of which the carburettor, magneto and engine were all stripped and cleaned. It took three days to complete the journey. The fault was eventually diagnosed as the cylinder-head warping when it got hot, allowing water into the cylinders. Once this had been remedied, the replacement lorry was fairly reliable, except for the fanbelt. Most fanbelts run between fan and engine, this one was ahead of the fan on a small pulley and due to a wobbly bearing it would keep flopping off. Often he would lose it on the way to Leighton Buzzard, and pick it up on the way back, this of course meant that it was forever boiling. He put a piece of wire netting underneath in the end to catch the belt, but before long the local garage had nicknamed him 'Fanbelt Teddy'. These old lorries consumed a gallon of 'Power' petrol every five miles, mind you it only cost 1*s.* 4*d.* a gallon in those days.

Below right: A Guy 50 cwt. lorry with drivers Ted Brantom and Jimmy Durrant in 1925.

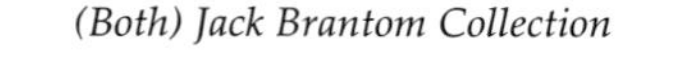
(Both) Jack Brantom Collection

A Leyland lorry owned by Joseph Arnold & Sons. *Frank Oakley*

No. 20 in H.G. Brown & Sons fleet was this Sentinel steam wagon. *Tom Lawson Collection*

An articulated sand lorry seen here at A.C. Biggs' depot.

Frank Oakley

A team photograph of A.C. Biggs' drivers. *Tom Lawson Collection*

Standard Gauge Link Lines

In an effort to overcome the serious problems of the local roads it was proposed that a standard gauge railway might be the answer. The railway would be constructed to link all the sand pits together and, at the same time join with the existing railway network. Proposals for such a scheme were first made in 1892 to the LNWR but were turned down.

In 1899, the idea for a Leighton Buzzard & Hitchin Light Railway went a step further with many in-depth plans being made. The proposals included many sidings along the route for the industries expected to build their premises beside the line, all of whom would of course require huge quantities of sand delivered to them. This route had the attraction of linking two main railway lines going northwards from London and would ensure lower transportation costs for Leighton Buzzard sand.

Despite enthusiasm for the scheme and a slightly modified version in 1902, attempts to build the railway ended in oblivion and the sand companies continued to pay huge amounts in compensation for the upkeep of the roads.

With the outbreak of World War I in 1914 there was a turning point in which the whole situation was completely reversed. Imported sand ceased to be a threat due to German occupation of Belgium. Leighton Buzzard sand was suddenly wanted in 'enormous quantities' by munition factories for the making of the means of mass destruction.

This huge increase in traffic left Leighton Buzzard each day by every available means of transport to satisfy the unquenchable demands of the

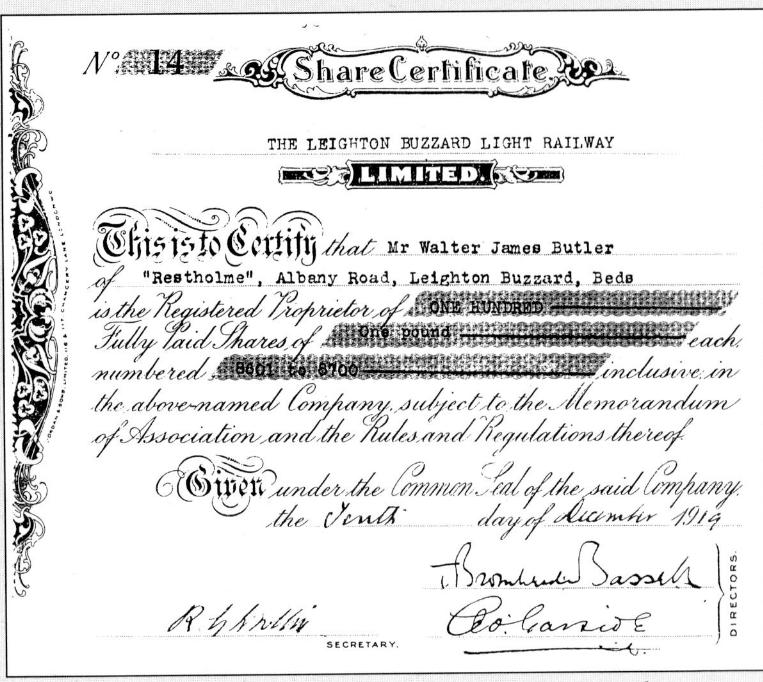

No. 14 Share Certificate.

THE LEIGHTON BUZZARD LIGHT RAILWAY

LIMITED.

This is to Certify that Mr Walter James Butler
of "Restholme", Albany Road, Leighton Buzzard, Beds
is the Registered Proprietor of ONE HUNDRED
Fully Paid Shares of One pound each
numbered 8601 to 8700 inclusive in
the above-named Company, subject to the Memorandum
of Association and the Rules and Regulations thereof.

Given under the Common Seal of the said Company
the Tenth day of December 1919

[signature] DIRECTORS.
[signature]
[signature] SECRETARY.

Two share certificates of the Leighton Buzzard Light Railway Ltd. The upper one dated 10th December, 1919, shows Walter James Butler, Arnold's quarry manager, purchasing 100 shares in the new railway. The lower one shows Joseph Arnold & Son's additional share holding after transfer to them of certificates held by the LBLR.

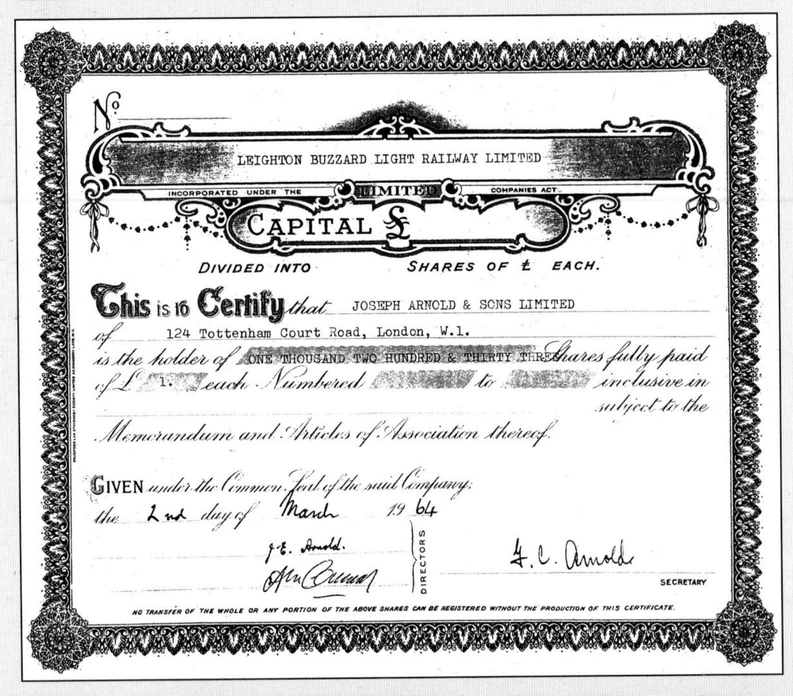

No.

LEIGHTON BUZZARD LIGHT RAILWAY LIMITED

INCORPORATED UNDER THE COMPANIES ACT

CAPITAL £

DIVIDED INTO SHARES OF £ EACH.

This is to Certify that JOSEPH ARNOLD & SONS LIMITED
of 124 Tottenham Court Road, London, W.1.
is the holder of ONE THOUSAND TWO HUNDRED & THIRTY THREE Shares fully paid
of £ 1. each Numbered to inclusive in
subject to the
Memorandum and Articles of Association thereof.

GIVEN under the Common Seal of the said Company
the 2nd day of March 1964

J.E. Arnold. DIRECTORS
[signature]
G. C. Arnold SECRETARY

NO TRANSFER OF THE WHOLE OR ANY PORTION OF THE ABOVE SHARES CAN BE REGISTERED WITHOUT THE PRODUCTION OF THIS CERTIFICATE.

munitions' factories. So important was the need for sand that the Government took over complete responsibility for the repairs of the roads for the duration of the War.

After the conflict the Government withdrew its commitment and as from January 1919 the sand companies were again forced to pay for the upkeep of the roads. This decision occurred at the time when greater output than ever before was needed, sand supplies from Europe were completely disrupted and new customers were queuing up all requiring sand to help rebuild the ravished economy of the country. With this in mind it became evident that the age of the train could not be put back any longer. Consequently in April 1919 Arnold's and Garside's put forward a plan for a 2 ft gauge railway to serve most of their interests.

Leighton Buzzard Light Railway

The route of the track would connect the operating quarries to the north of Leighton Buzzard, avoiding the town to the east and deliver the sand direct to the washing and drying plants of the two companies in Billington Road. Thereafter the sand would leave for onward shipment to its eventual destinations via the Grovebury Road sidings and the Dunstable standard gauge branch line. After obtaining approval from the Urban District Council to construct nine ungated level crossings, the Leighton Buzzard Light Railway Ltd was duly incorporated in July 1919 as a private company with a nominal capital of £20,000 in £1 shares.

Construction of the railway started in August 1919 and proceeded extremely rapidly. Indeed all records appear to have been broken as it was completed by November just four months later. Three and one quarter miles of track were laid and ready for operation. However, it later transpired that the work had been 'bodged', a lighter 25 lb. rail being laid instead of the 30 lb. specified. Straight rails, sprung into place, were used on the curves; contractors, Lamb & Phillips, certainly knew how to cut corners. The brief to the constructor was to avoid steep hills and sharp bends, however one section of the line contains a gradient of 1 in 25 and two extremely sharp curves were included. These obstacles still plague the line today but certainly add interest to the journey. The bill for the work totalled £12,030 13*s*. 6*d*.

It was originally conceived that the line would be horse-drawn but negotiations were well in hand in May 1919 for the purchase of two surplus War Department Hudswell, Clarke steam engines Nos. 1377 and 1378 from Robert Hudson Ltd of Leeds. The locomotives were destined to serve in the Italian Campaign but were not delivered before the Armistice.

In view of this type of locomotive's performance in France and Flanders in World War I it was calculated that these steam engines would be ideal for haulage of sand on the LBLR. The locomotives were purchased for the sum of £1,225 each and were delivered to Leighton Buzzard in time for the opening ceremony of the line on the 20th November, 1919. Four photographs exist of this event, two of which picture the steam engines - unfortunately they are

UNDER GOVERNMENT CONTROL.

TELEPHONE: 20004 & 20005
TELEGRAMS: RAILTRUX, LEEDS.
CODES USED A B C 5TH EDITION AND PRIVATE CODE IN OUR CATALOGUE.

CONTRACTORS TO THE WAR OFFICE, ADMIRALTY, INDIA OFFICE, CROWN AGENTS FOR THE COLONIES, H.M. OFFICE OF WORKS, COLONIAL & FOREIGN GOVERNMENTS, ETC.

LONDON OFFICE: SUFFOLK HOUSE CANNON STREET E.C.
LONDON TELEPHONE: 3162 CITY.

Robert Hudson Ltd.

WORKS
GILDERSOME FOUNDRY, NEAR LEEDS.
SIDINGS: GILDERSOME, G.N. RLY.

HEAD OFFICES:
38A, BOND STREET, LEEDS.

MANUFACTURERS OF PORTABLE & PERMANENT LIGHT RAILWAYS. SWITCHES. CROSSINGS. TURNTABLES. LOCOMOTIVES. ROLLING STOCK. STEEL TIP WAGONS. SUGAR CANE CARS. NITRATE CARS. MINING TRUCKS. COLLIERY TUBS. WHEELS & AXLES. ETC.

May 9th 1919.

PLEASE REPLY TO HEAD OFFICES AND QUOTE OUR REFERENCE. } Ref. "H" Dept.E. 16443.

Messrs Joseph Arnold & Sons,
124, Tottenham Court Road,
LONDON. W.1.

Dear Sirs:-

STEAM LOCOMOTIVES.

We beg to thank you for your letter of the 8th of May. We enclose herewith one of our Loco Catalogues, the Engine you refer to is to codeword "POUTAGAN" on page 19 but to suit 600 m.m. Rail Gauge (23.5/8").

The Engines are complete in every respect with Copper Firebox, and absolutely identical with large quantities we have supplied for Military purposes. We have 3 of these Engines in stock at the present moment which we are prepared to sell at the special price of:-

£1225- 0- 0 each Nett f.o.t. Leeds.

The current cost for replacing today is over £1400- 0- 0. We have offered them to 2 or 3 of our friends and we expect they will be sold during the next few days, we had 4 in stock and sold one yesterday. If these Locos are likely to interest you we should be pleased if you would let us know at once ~~and~~ as we might at any rate be able to let you have the first refusal of one of them.

Yours faithfully,
ROBERT HUDSON LIMITED

E. Hudson DIRECTOR.

E/- Loco Ctg.

covered in bunting and are obscured by 35 invited guests who became the first-ever passengers to journey along the line. They rode in specially built carriages hauled by the contractor's petrol-driven locomotive.

The steam engines did not have a happy life at Leighton Buzzard, being blamed for numerous derailments on the curves where the straight lengths of track were bent into use. The locomotives were also responsible for setting fire to the untreated sleepers provided by local timber merchant H.G. Brown from nearby woodland. The engines were also notorious for depositing horrible black smuts all over the sand they were hauling behind them.

Both Hudswell, Clarkes had small water tanks, only holding 110 gallons, this meant that they had to halt *en route* at Swing Swang Bridge to replenish supplies from the Clipstone Brook flowing below. This extra top up enabled the engines to get their loads from one end of the line to the other. The troublesome locomotives were sold together in August 1920 to R.H. Neal & Co. for the total sum of £1,150.

The steam engines were quickly replaced by petrol-powered locomotives, an example of which was used by the contractor to build the line originally and hauled the opening day special train. The sand companies must have been impressed by its efficient performance and easy running and so others were ordered for use on the LBLR. This type of petrol locomotive was used extensively behind the Western Front in World War I to ferry supplies and equipment forward to the front line, returning with the dead and dying. The locomotives were built by Motor Rail and Tram Car Co. Ltd of Bedford. The 'Simplex' as it was known was an immediate success at Leighton Buzzard and from that first day until now, their distinctive Dorman engines have never stopped ticking over. Many of the Simplexes were shipped back to the UK as surplus war equipment, these machines being available then at reduced costs to the LBLR for hauling sand instead of shells.

Initially two sizes were built by Motor Rail, 20 hp and 40 hp. The smaller cabless version had bow-shaped frames. At first three of these were purchased by the LBLR to work alongside the horses. Later they would traditionally be found working in the sand quarries, where their duties consisted of shunting filled skips from the sand face up the steep gradients out of pits, to the sidings feeding the main line.

In comparison the 40 hp variants were massive monsters. Depending on their role in the War these engines were available in three types; open, protected or armoured. The armour-plated variety was practically a tank on rails having a tiny slot for the driver to peer through. At Leighton Buzzard six 40 hp Simplexes operated along the main line hauling skips back and forth. They weighed 6 tons and quickly used the 20 gallons of petrol they held in their fuel tanks.

Records show two other 40 hp engines were purchased in addition to the six above, seemingly to be used for spares, they were never seen running on the main line. The 40 hp locomotives were eventually cut up for scrap in 1959 after 40 years of excellent service.

The LBLR steam engines wait patiently with shareholders, dignitaries and honoured guests for speeches to begin to mark the opening of the LBLR on 20th November, 1919.

Alan Keef Collection

The first passenger train on the narrow gauge railway at Leighton Buzzard, complete with Union Jack at the tail. Thirty-five guests from the opening ceremony were hauled along the line by the contractor's petrol locomotive. *Tom Lawson Collection*

One of the Hudswell, Clarke 0-6-0 well tanks is in steam at Billington Road engine shed. Contractor's locomotive Works No. MR 1856 is also rostered for duty. A well was dug in the yard for the thirsty locomotives to take on water. *Author's Collection*

Billington Road depot *c.* 1922 with 40 hp armoured and protected locomotives on display together with two 20 hp Motor Rails. The left-hand one is MR 1757. *Chris Daniels Collection*

LBLR No. 2 at Billington Road in November 1945. *Arthur Wells*

Six-ton armoured Simpex, LBLR No. 3 runs round at Stanbridge Road loop. The plating on the locomotive was sufficient to withstand shrapnel whilst they worked behind the trenches during World War I. *Bill Smith*

LBLR No. 3, MR 478 (WD 2199) passes Abraham's Farm on 8th April, 1954. *Geoffrey Starmer*

A 1954 view of LBLR No. 4 with crew, *left to right*, Fred Turney (fitter), Dicky Alder, Trevor Roff, Ken Quick, Kevin Newton, and Ray Turney.

Trevor Roff

Early Leighton Buzzard Light Railway Locomotives

Hudswell, Clarke Steam Engines

Type	*Works No.*	*Built*	*War Dept Light Railway No.*
0-6-0 well tank	HC 1377	1918	3207
0-6-0 well tank	HC 1378	1918	3208

Early 20 hp Petrol Simplexes

Type	*Works No.*	*Built*	*War Dept Light Railway No.*
4 wheel petrol	MR 1856	1918	(contractor's loco)
4 wheel petrol	MR 1757	1918	2478
4 wheel petrol	MR 2213	1924	2406

40 hp Petrol Armoured/Protected Simplexes

LBLR No.	*Type*	*Works No.*	*Built*	*War Dept Light Railway No.*
1	4 wheel petrol	MR 3674	1924	2316
2	4 wheel petrol	MR 1383	1918	3104
3	4 wheel petrol	MR 478	1918	2199
4	4 wheel petrol	MR 468	1918	2189
5	4 wheel petrol	MR 3848	1934	2228
6	4 wheel petrol	MR 1299	1918	3020
	4 wheel petrol	MR 3675	1924	3005
	4 wheel petrol	MR 1283	1918	3004

Over the years the petrol locomotives were gradually replaced by more efficient diesel-powered Motor Rails, more and more kept on arriving at Leighton Buzzard until at one stage more than 100 of these small, squat and to some, ugly, dark green locomotives had been delivered. Many of these sturdy Simplexes could be seen each day double-heading fully-laden skips out of the sand quarries whilst other locomotives bustled around, fussing to and fro, in attendance in case bankers were needed. Yet more diesels shunted empties up to the sand face ready for refilling by draglines or Ruston-Bucyrus face shovels. The principal task of the 20 hp diesels was to feed skip after skip to the main line where the 40 hp locomotives took over. Many, however, ventured off the branch lines onto the the LBLR track to deliver sand to local industries.

Both Arnold's and Garside's operated their own locomotive fleets within their own quarries, whilst the LBLR, jointly owned by the two sand companies, ran its engines over the main line. Since its formation the LBLR owned no less than 21 locomotives; in 1958 when only six modern main line diesel engines were left under its control a re-organisation took place with each company being responsible for its own main line locomotives. These were divided up with four becoming numbers 41, 42, 43 and 44, going to Joseph Arnold & Son and the remaining two, being numbered 10 and 12, going to George Garside's patronage. The Light Railway operated afterwards by charging a toll to each company related to the tonnage of sand hauled over the main line section.

With the quarries packed with 20 hp Simplexes it often became necessary to transfer these locomotives from pit to pit as business dictated, this made the

LBLR No. 6, MR 1299 (WD 3020) awaits right of way at Double Arches *c*. 1920. The horse will take the empty skips back into the quarry.
Joseph Arnold & Sons Ltd

engines increasingly difficult to identify as every one was in dark green livery and with white wooden window frames. To sort out the situation Arnold's numbered their locomotives on the bonnets and also on the apex of the cab roofs. Garside's locomotives also had a numeral stencilled on the bonnets but in addition the company had the delightful idiosyncrasy of naming their locomotives after racehorses that had won the Derby or Grand National, and other important races.

One would have thought that this must have made life easier for keeping maintenance records in order, however, the bonnets tended to be swapped around so that locomotives went through a phase of being one name and re-appearing, later, as another. It did not help, either, that names were also changed to fit in with the latest winner of a race, the same numbered engine going through its paces under two or three different names.

The decline of the Light Railway, which hauled 100,000 tons of sand traffic in its most prosperous years, started in 1955 when the national railway strike of that year forced the sand companies to turn to road transport. Lorries had been collecting bagged sand for many years, inevitably the decision was taken that in future more deliveries would be dispatched by road to guarantee supplies for customers.

By the early 1960s the Light Railway had become increasingly run by Arnold's, therefore it was not surprising that by 1964 the company became the sole owners of the LBLR. Arnold's built a new washery at the northern end of the line at Double Arches and directed lorries to this site thus leaving little traffic for the railway to carry. Finally what sand was still being sent away via the standard gauge railway sidings at Billington Road ceased in 1969 when British Rail closed the remnants of the Leighton Buzzard to Dunstable branch line. Operation on the Light Railway lingered on at a much reduced scale with sand now spasmodically heading northwards from Chamberlain's Barn.

Simplex diesels which proudly worked the whole network of the railway could now be found lying abandoned everywhere, hidden amongst overgrown grass and shrubs. No more could the clanking of skips be heard as they rattled along spilling sand either side of them. The only sound which was audible was the scrap man as he cut up the unwanted locomotives and wagons. A good number, did however, find new homes elsewhere in the country earning a living in other industries.

In 1981 the last vestige of the once vast system was the production at Garside's Munday's Hill Quarry. Here Ruston 10 RB shovels were still loading skips. The last five working 20 hp diesels, *Arkle, Ayala, Damredub, Mill Reef* and *Red Rum,* with their engines beating fast, then hauled the sand out of the quarry, to trundle over a short stretch of the Leighton Buzzard Light Railway to Garside's Eastern Way plant.

The little hard working Simplexes were replaced by a dumper truck.

Having a rest at the bottom of Marley's bank. *Left to right*: Ron Read, Jack Major, Bill Smith, Tom Jones and young Saunders. *Bill Smith Collection*

Lunch time at Double Arches. *Left to right*: Dick Webb, David Showler, unknown and Fred Webb. *Tom Lawson Collection*

Scratch the surface soil around Leighton Buzzard and very soon you will discover sand beneath your feet. This well known fact was used to advantage by many builders in the town who used to construct vast numbers of houses in the area with cellars.

Having obtained the plot of land the first task the contractors did was to dig a big hole, from this, they obtained all the sand they needed to build the house as well as creating the cellar which made the property more valuable.

In the later years of the sand industry it was from houses like these that the ammophiles (sand lovers) used to cycle or walk to work each day, a distance of no more than a few miles. In earlier years the men were either employed as 'dobbers' that is those that used to work on the sand face or as horse men or boys. After modernisation they became excavator drivers, locomotive drivers and engine boys. The main job of the engine boys was to flag the locomotives over the ungated level crossings.

From the beginning it was common practice that sons followed their fathers into the sand pits after leaving school at fourteen; the lads had the responsibility of looking after the horses or became engine boys when the locomotives arrived on the scene.

Like boys everywhere they all acquired nicknames which stuck with them throughout their lives; 'Shrimp', 'Digger', 'Popeye', 'Yatty', 'Shady', 'Pigeon' and 'Shunty' are some remembered. When they became men at 21 most remained together working as a gang at the sand face, thus building up close and firm friendships.

As a horse boy in 1926 Arthur Shales nicknamed 'Bunk' earned 15 shillings a week. To do this he walked two miles to work each day arriving at 5 am at the stables. The first job was to light a fire and draw some water from the well. By 5.30 am he had made the tea, which was eagerly drunk by Mr Capp the postman who called in at this time to deliver the mail.

During the next 30 minutes Arthur used to clean and polish the harnesses of his horse 'George', before leading him to Double Arches Quarry in time for the dobbers to start filling their skips full of sand. The men toiled from 6.30 am until 5 pm; four horses were used at Double Arches, other steeds were used elsewhere in different pits.

At Double Arches 'George' led by Arthur used to haul one skip at a time full of sand from the quarry face up out of the pit to the sidings at the end of the LBLR main line. Here the train was marshalled ready for its journey to Billington Road.

At the age of 21 Arthur became a 'dobber', cutting sand by hand and filling skips at the quarry face. Wages were much better but these depended on how many wagons were filled. Since this was piece work a foreman kept a strict record of output. One of the foreman was known as 'Stand-Up', not because he was a comedian but because he used to stand over the men all day, keeping a watchful eye on production. Dobbers, by the very nature of their work, were exposed to all types of weather conditions and were required to fill a minimum of 30 skips per day. If the weather turned really bad however, they were allowed to shelter in the quarry hut to play cards and chat until things improved. A low hourly rate was paid in these instances.

Amongst the many specific orders his team had to fulfil Arthur remembers

Arnold's petrol engined No.7 stands at the quarry face with a rake of skips ready to be filled by a gang of 'dobbers' on a sunny day in 1940.
Joseph Arnold & Sons Ltd

they had to provide over 200 tons of pure white sand per day for Pilkington Glass. Also he recalls digging thousands of tons for the 'sand blasting' of London's buildings in the big clean up after the smog.

Arthur received a clock from Arnold's after he completed 25 years' service and an engraved watch when he reached his 50th year for the company.

Although he could have carried on working in the quarries during World War II, his job being a reserved occupation, he decided it was only right and loyal to fight for his country during this period, a decision which severely affected his pension.

Amongst Arthur's gang at Double Arches during his long stay there were the following dobbers:

Jimmy Giltrow - foreman	David Showler	Joey Osbourne
Les Rutland	Tom Woolhead	Jack Showler
Bill Axton	George Ensby	Cyril Galloway
Les Pantling	Tom Woodcroft	George Deverill

* *

Alan Tearle began his life with the LBLR in 1941 joining as an engine / flag boy working with Andrew Stone who was the driver of a fully armoured Simplex. Two years later in 1943 he left to enrol in the Royal Navy.

After his 'demob' in 1947 he joined the Light Railway again, this time as one of the drivers of the armoured and protected petrol Simplexes on the main line. In 1954 he was allocated a modern 40 hp diesel to drive, this was No. 11 which arrived new from Motor Rail in Bedford. (This locomotive MR 10409, became No. 43 in 1958 when Arnold's took control of the LBLR.) At this time Ray Turney was his flag boy.

Alan used to cycle to the engine sheds at Billington Road to commence work at 6.30 am. By then one train had already left, departing at 6 am to take empty skips to Double Arches in order that the sand dobbers could begin loading immediately they arrived for work at the quarry.

At around 6.30 am three Arnold's and two Garside's trains left Billington Road hauling empties, 30 skips each was the average but Alan's engine would often take up to 40 as it weighed 6 tons and had a 3-speed gearbox.

After the first trip, loaded, to Billington Road, all the drivers had breakfast cooked on the workshop's pot-bellied stove. The meal was cooked by the crew of the 6 am train who were obviously the first to arrive back; the meal consisted of eggs, bacon and mashed potato cooked in billy cans.

The LBLR main line was always very busy, with each driver making four round trips per day from Double Arches to Billington Road; each journey would take 1¼ hours providing nothing held up the train. Often, bagged dry sand was loaded onto ex-War Department bogie wagons at Double Arches, when this occurred, they counted as the equivalent of four skips and were always marshalled next to the engine.

When returning with empties a driver always had to give way to an approaching loaded train so a sharp look-out was kept for trains coming towards them from Double Arches. These could often be spotted over one mile away as much of the line ran through open fields. The driver of the empty train

Bill Smith (*left*) and Vic Hart take a short break at Arnold's. The unusual shape of the handrail of the locomotive they are leaning on suggests that this is one of Arnold's departures from the Motor Rail tradition and was probably built by the London firm of F.C. Hibberd. *Owen Roberts*

would invariably have plenty of time to enter the nearest loop, even if this meant reversing some distance. A game of football usually ensued to pass the time or if the stop happened to be at Leedon Loop the crew used to go rabbiting or pick the excellent mushrooms in Jack Heady's field.

Stops were frequent as there were also up to 14 trains of 10 skips per day going into Marley Roof Tiles beside Stanbridge Road, these were hauled by the lighter 20 hp Simplexes.

Further north at Co-op Loop traffic from Arnold's Chamberlains Barn Quarry entered the main line system. Stonehenge Brickworks and the adjacent Dri-Roof Tileworks also received regular deliveries of sand to their respective sidings. Nine Acre Quarry also had a connection here. Lastly came the output from Munday's Hill Quarry which sometimes interfered with the routine.

Delays were also caused at some of the level crossings which had gates across the track to prevent horses, cattle and sheep escaping from the fields. These were opened and closed by the flag boy.

There were many floods to contend with along the route of the light railway, the most serious used to occur at Alder's Herb Fields (Three-penny Bit Curve). Each time there was a heavy downpour the embankment was washed away and the track was left in mid-air. A platelayer's hut was located nearby for the Permanent Way (PW) man, Harry Jeffs, to carry out repairs. Another PW hut was situated at Bryan's Loop, this was named after the man who was in charge of the maintenance over this section of the line. At the Double Arches end of the line yet another hut could be found. Due to the number of trains using the Eastern Way level crossing a permanent flagman was stationed there, when the weather deteriorated he would pop into the shelter and have a cup of tea.

Winter conditions also brought problems, braking was extremely difficult in the snow, it was very hard to stop the trains with so much weight behind them when going down hill. Brakes often had to be applied 100 yards or more from where you wanted to stop. In severe frost or icy conditions the engines were often chained to the track to stop them sliding and creeping away by themselves.

Alan Tearle was very proud of his locomotive and made sure it was the cleanest engine on the line; he left the Leighton Buzzard Light Railway in 1955.

* *

Vic Hart was an engine driver for George Garside's. In 1945 his son Derek followed his father into the sand industry, joining as a flag boy after leaving school at the age of 15. He remembers that there were six boys in total riding on the main line engines and that they would report to work in Billington Road at 6 am in the summer and 7 am in the winter. His main duty was to stop road traffic at the ungated level crossings by holding up a red flag or alteranatively waving a red lamp if conditions were dark or foggy.

In his first year, Derek was involved in a head-on collision between two trains, in the early morning mist, at the top of the hill north of Stonehenge Brickworks. Both engines careered off the track, passed through a hedge to end up in Miletree Road. Most of the skips followed, causing an awful pile up. Derek and the flag boy on the other locomotive managed to jump clear just before the crash but both engine drivers stayed in their cabs and were fortunate to come out of the accident

'Knocking off time' at Double Arches Quarry with dobbers, Joey Osbourne, George 'Digger' Deverill, Freddy Bardon, James Turney and Colin Stevens.

Chris Daniels Collection

unhurt. A whole day's distribution was affected whilst the track was repaired.

Travelling southwards from Double Arches the LBLR makes a 90 degree bend at Co-op Loop. At this spot the flag boys used to jump off the engine and sprint across the apex of the bend to bring road traffic to a halt before the train reached Vandyke Road level crossing. The locomotive drivers never slowed down approaching the road as they were afraid the engine might get stuck on the check rails protecting the tight curve. After going over the level crossing some of the flag boys used to hop onto the back of the train and then climb onto the sand. As the train continued its journey towards 'Swing-Swang' bridge they would leap from skip to skip to rejoin their engine.

Riding in the 40 hp armoured Simplex left much to be desired, in the summer months Derek used to sit on the engine's tool box to keep cool but in the freezing depths of winter changed position to be next to the warmth of the radiator.

Derek's ambition was to follow in his father's footsteps and become an engine driver, by riding on the engines all day he had learnt what and what not to do. Derek longed for the day when he would be in charge of his own train, however, due to an incident on the infamous Marley's Bank his dream did not come true.

Nightmares on Marley's Bank

From the outset of the LBLR the 1 in 25 gradient of Marley's Bank was feared the most, named after Marley Roof Tiles whose factory the line disected, the ascent caused many headaches over the years. Problems were not helped by a siding which left the main line part way up to enter the company's yard.

The notorious incline claimed numerous victims as fully laden trains struggled to gain the semblance of safety at Stanbridge Road Loop. Difficulties were as a matter of course exacerbated in the winter months. It would have been nice for the engine drivers to take a run up the severe bank but fate had decreed that the line should have an extremely sharp, blind curve, right at the bottom to catch out the unwary.

A large tree also masked the way ahead before the throttle could be eased open. Knowing the right amount of adhesion to apply to the wheels for the steep climb ahead really tested the driver's ability, whether they be in one of the big 40 hp petrol locomotives or a modern diesel.

From a very early stage the practice of dividing the trains was adopted, this occurred at Leedon Loop where the 24 skips of sand heading towards Billington Road were split into two halves. The procedure made life much easier and at the same time had the additional bonus of putting less strain on the couplings between the wagons. Despite the precautions links still snapped causing dangerous and un-controlled breakaways to charge headlong down the bank and derail on the bend below. This caused chaos as skip after skip piled on top of each other. Those wagons that managed to negotiate the curve carried on under their own momentum to eventually reach a 'dud' point specifically installed to halt their further progress down the line. The 'dud' point was always set so that runaways woud discard their loads of sand into a field, this meant that all loaded trains from the quarries had to stop whilst the flag boy switched the lever over for main line running. Alan Tearle recalls that 'overtime' could sometimes be earned on Saturdays and Sundays shovelling the sand from these spillages back into skips, that is if he was not needed to help slew the track closer to the working face in the quarries. Locomotive drivers were encouraged to check the couplings for cracks and any other signs of deterioration, but needless to say, this was often a casual glance and so runaways occurred more often than would be expected.

There were so many trains following each other along the main line that it became common practice for the following train to leave all its skips at Leedon Loop whilst the locomotive gave 'banking' assistance to the entire train in front. This method of working obviously avoided the need to divide the skips into two halves. The new cycle of operating was often repeated and enabled trains to ascend Marley's Bank in one swift and simple movement. At particularly busy times a locomotive was allocated for banking duties only.

Often at the end of the day the first locomotive to return to Billington Road used to go back 'light engine' to Leedon Loop and sit in the trap point waiting for the final trains to pass, each time it acted as a banker pushing the heavily loaded wagons to the upper part of the section. Those trains that had to be divided at Leedon Loop and taken up Marley's Bank in two parts were re-formed in the loop at Stanbridge Road. Here the first half of the train would have been left 'spragged' or secured with a metal bar through the wheels of the last skip. Re-connecting the loaded trains was an extremely hazardous operation. It was here that the majority of accidents on the LBLR took place. For the most part, tops of fingers were crushed and fingernails blackened when fly shunting skips or in using sprags to brake the trains. However, others were more severe, in one case causing the loss of a leg and in another instance a fatality.

In 1947, just two years after he started work, Derek Hart suffered an accident in icy conditions at Stanbridge Road Loop. It happened when he was attempting to pull out a connecting pin between two locomotives. Derek suddenly slipped as he reached across the buffers and was crushed by the engines. He was rushed to hospital where it was diagnosed that he had a fractured pelvis and a badly injured hip which caused great pain to the base of his spine. It took Derek 15 months to recover.

The tracks of the light railway start by the exchange sidings at Billington Road where skips of sand are emptied from a tipping dock into standard gauge wagons. English Electric Type '4' (later class '40') No. D299 shunts empty sand wagons into position ready for filling either side of the Arnold's loading gantry. The old brickworks buildings and the Dunstable branch can be seen in the background, August 1968. *Chris Daniels*

The last ever revenue earning train on the Leighton Buzzard-Dunstable branch. Brush type '4' (later class '47') No. D1672 *Colossus* is seen at Arnold's Billington Road Sidings on 5th December, 1969, the former tipping dock lies partly dismantled on the left. *Kevin Lane*

Description of the Line in 1960

by Alan Keef

The tracks of the Light Railway start by Arnold's exchange sidings at Billington Road. Here skips are emptied from a loading dock into standard gauge wagons. Three lines then cross the road in parallel, one line eventually going on into Pratt's Pit, whilst the others fan out northwards in a variety of loops and spurs. On the far side of the loops is a long siding where empty skips are stocked overnight and at weekends.

Beside the road is a large locomotive shed, 110 ft x 40 ft constructed in 1950. The building is substantially built in brick with stores and offices on one side. At the far end are the workshops where the engines receive their major repairs. The locomotive shed must be one of the most palatial ever owned by a light railway company, it houses a total of 20 locomotives.

Beyond the shed is a small rusty corrugated iron building, which in earlier days acted as a maintenance shop. At this point the loops converge into a single track to climb at a steady 1 in 45 to be joined by a further branch line used by George Garside's. This track makes a trailing connection to cross Billington Road again. The line leads to Garside's washing and bagging plants. In the complex of buildings can be found an engine shed and beyond some loading docks. An old locomotive dump exists nearby.

Further up the main line are the three original LBLR sheds (1919-1946). Built of corrugated iron, one shed held three locomotives on three separate roads whilst another longer shed held two engines on a single road. Rail connection has been broken and all tracks lifted.

Continuing on, for a further 50 yards, the line curves sharply round to the east as the gradient steepens noticeably to about 1 in 25, a look backwards shows another branch. This line descends to Arnold's principal washing and grading facilities at an even steeper gradient, to go over Billington Road once more. Having crossed the road, the line turns sharply right in to the washery. This horrendous section of the railway is extremely busy with skips full of sand going back and forth almost continuously. Trains are worked down this slope with an engine at either end, meanwhile a man stands in the road with a red flag or stop board. Above the descent, a lifting barrier, made out of old rail, has been installed to prevent trains and skips stored overnight further up the track from running down the bank.

Hereafter the two loops are formed, one on either side of the main line. These are used by loaded trains waiting clearance to carry on with the final stage of their journey, either to the washers or exchange sidings. Arnold's used the loop adjacent to Page's Park and Garside's the one nearest Pratt's Pit. Once the train was secured in the appropriate siding, the 40 hp locomotive would leave in pursuit of empty skips for the return trip and a 20 hp engine would be dispatched to take the train, six skips at a time into the various plants.

From around 1958 when the locomotives were split between Arnold's and Garside's, different geometric symbols (a triangle, stripe, rectangle, circle or cross etc.) were painted on their cabs to enable identification of the train at a distance. This sign language enabled the correct company's 20 hp Simplex to be sent out to meet the train and offer braking assistance if required.

Going on, the line singles again and gently curves to the left, climbing gradually at 1 in 69 before levelling out by a red brick barn with an accommodation crossing. This is followed by another - although only occasionally used - passing and storage loop.

Once past the loop, the line begins to dip fairly steeply. At the bottom of the gradient a footpath crosses the railway between the RAF married quarters and the precincts of RAF Stanbridge. In the first years of the Light Railway there was a gated crossing here but the track has been raised over the years so that it is about the height of the gate posts, still in the hedge! A footbridge was built in 1962.

From this position the railway starts to climb again until a siding leads off to the right into the works of the Leighton Buzzard Concrete Company. During each working day a locomotive had to deliver 3 or 6 skips of sand, into the confined area of the compound, along the short stretch of track. The operation involved shunting across the ungated Stanbridge Road level crossing. Discharged skips were collected by a train going back to the quarries later.

Just a short distance further on the railway parts again to form another loop. Stanbridge Road Loop is one of the most important on the railway, loaded skips would be left ready to be linked up again after being divided prior to the 1 in 25 gradient of Marley's Bank. From Stanbridge Road the line starts to descend extremely rapidly getting more precipitous all the time until it seems to disappear altogether down the 1 in 25 drop through the middle of Marley Roof Tiles. Here there are whistle boards and 'Beware of the Train' signs in various languages positioned on the works' crossing into the factory.

At one time a siding served Marley Roof Tiles from this location, it must have seen tremendous use for very nearly half of the light railway traffic never went beyond this point, but ended up being off-loaded straight into the tile works yard for immediate use.

Marley's Bank has a bad reputation, it was very tricky to ascend and drivers learnt very quickly from experience the arts involved in reaching the top. Many tales of runaways were told caused by violent jerks snapping the couplings of the skips. Once the crew of a following train only just managed to jump clear as a rake of fully laden skips piled high onto their locomotive. Prayers of thanks were offered to the Gods and extra health insurance taken out afterwards.

Our journey continues onwards to Leedon Loop, the major crossing point on the railway. Trains were broken down into two parts here to help ease the struggle of climbing Marley's Bank. Just ahead the line goes over Hockliffe Road level crossing and then runs beside hedgerows, dead straight, before reaching a long sweeping dog-legged curve on an embankment (Three-penny Bit Curve). Here the skips would jolt savagely as they proceeded over the joints in the track.

Eventually Clipstone Brook is reached, this is crossed by a substantial brick and girder bridge of 15 ft span, known as Swing Swang after the adjacent thoroughfare. The track proceeds directly ahead rising at 1 in 45 to the Co-op Field crossing (Vandyke Road), where a platelayer's hut stands beside the gate on the far side.

Once across the road the railway swings to the right on a long and very sharp check-railed curve. Just before the track straightens, a trailing siding has been laid for empty trains to reverse into. By facing points, the Chamberlain's Barn branch leaves the main line to turn sharp left here and almost immediately becomes a loop. This loop is completely overgrown and half buried, although both pairs of points are still in place. The branch heads straight between high hedges on either side, the way only being kept open by the passage of trains to and from Chamberlain's Barn Quarry.*

* In 1964 a new branch line linking Chamberlain's Barn to New Trees Quarry was laid down across open fields and through a cutting. This crossed Shenley Hill Road before reaching the new workings.

Returning to the main line it now runs inside a hedge and ditch alongside Vandyke road climbing all the time at 1 in 68; two field crossings are encountered along this stretch of track until at the summit the railway eases off to form another loop. Bryan's Loop is the busiest on the railway and is much longer than most of the others on the line.

At the next field crossing there is another platelayer's hut traditionally built in corrugated iron. From here the line gradually descends for quite a distance to reach Shenley Hill crossing. After the crossing, the track runs straight under the canopy of some large elm trees and then between a hedge and a fence past Stonehenge Brick Works. Along this section there are numerous sidings, spurs and loops together with loading bays to the left-hand side of the main line going into the works yard. Beyond the brickworks a branch goes off back through the yard again to Nine Acre Pit which lies behind the works.

Leaving this point the railway climbs continuously through a cutting on the side of a 1 in 47 hill for quite a long distance. Halfway up, the main line divides into an extensive section of double track. As soon as the line singles again, another branch line is encountered leading to Garside's Munday's Hill Quarry. Beyond lies Garside's repair shops, and a loading gantry.

Eventually we come to the final road crossing over Eastern Way to Double Arches where the line forks, the left-hand road leading to Arnold's quarries and the right-hand to Garside's Churchway Quarry.

Splintering away from the LBLR main line, lighter 20 lb. track, often with Jubilee tin plate sleepers, continued for distances of one mile or more down into the quarries. Near to the working face the line would branch again into a 'Y' to allow empties to be shunted whilst another train of skips was being loaded with sand. As the working face was eroded back the track had to be slewed closer to the bank of sand to make loading easier.

Arnold's bow-framed locomotive No. 4 stands on the transfer ramp at Billington Road with two 10 ton dropside bogie wagons delivering bagged sand on 16th February, 1959. The three row brick pillar construction supporting steel girders can be clearly seen in this view of the gantry. On top of the girders sleepers were laid to which two tracks were fixed. *F.A. Blencowe*

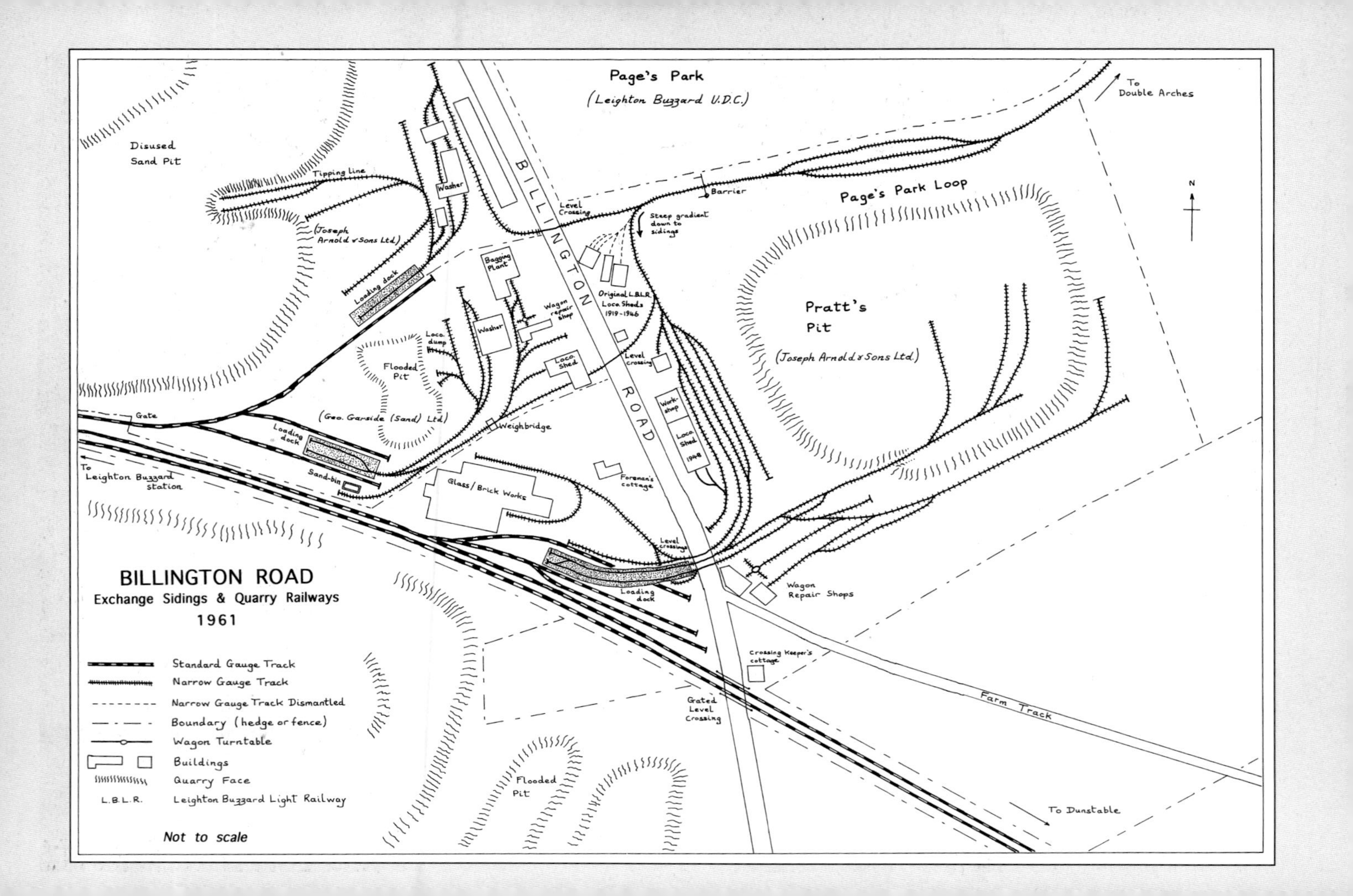

BILLINGTON ROAD
Exchange Sidings & Quarry Railways
1961
Page's Park
(Leighton Buzzard U.D.C.)
To Double Arches
Page's Park Loop
Barrier
N
Level Crossing
Steep gradient down to sidings
Pratt's Pit
(Joseph Arnold & Sons Ltd.)
Disused Sand Pit
Tipping line
Washer
(Joseph Arnold & Sons Ltd)
Loading dock
Bagging Plant
Wagon repair shop
Washer
Loco. dump
Flooded Pit
Loco. Shed
Original L.B.L.R. Loco. Sheds 1919-1946
Level crossing
Work-shop
Loco. Shed 1948
(Geo. Garside (Sand) Ltd)
Weighbridge
Gate
Loading dock
To Leighton Buzzard station
Sand-bin
Glass / Brick Works
Foreman's cottage
Level crossing
Loading dock
Wagon Repair Shops
Crossing Keeper's cottage
Gated Level Crossing
Farm Track
Flooded Pit
To Dunstable
Standard Gauge Track
Narrow Gauge Track
Narrow Gauge Track Dismantled
Boundary (hedge or fence)
Wagon Turntable
Buildings
Quarry Face
L.B.L.R. Leighton Buzzard Light Railway
Not to scale

Arnold's private owner wagons stand beside the newly constructed tipping dock *c.* 1934. The Leighton Buzzard to Dunstable branch and Billington Road (standard gauge) level crossing are in the background. *Joseph Arnold & Sons Ltd*

Further along Billington Road was situated George Garside (Sand) Company's complex. This comprehensive site consisted of a locomotive shed, washer, and a bagging plant. They also had an exchange siding here for main line shipments. On 2nd February, 1959, cabless Garside Simplexes *Devon Loch* and *Honeylight* await their drivers, who are probably watching the passing steam engine going by on the Dunstable branch. *F.A. Blencowe*

Arnold's No. 4 on the plethora of sidings near the transfer ramp, 14th December, 1957. No doubt Alf Eggleton, the Arnold's foreman, parked the locomotive here while he had his dinner in the cottage behind, where he lived. Alf called the locomotive 'Gertie'. *F.A. Blencowe*

Doutelle stands ready for action on the steep section of the Garside's transfer ramp. It was obviously a quiet day on 2nd February, 1959. *F.A. Blencowe*

It is almost possible to hear the noise of the machinery and hammering coming from Garside's wagon repair shops on 8th January, 1960. Mr Webb, still wearing his raincoat, is busy grinding wheel sets. *Sydney Leleux*

Garside's locomotive *Ribot* stands, ticking over, outside the locomotive shed. *LBNGR Archives*

Billington Road washery in 1930. In the background stands the standard gauge siding on a wooden pier with the Leighton Buzzard Glass Co. factory in the distance. *Arnold White PLC*

The last remains of the wooden pier and narrow gauge tipping line in 1958. Standard gauge sidings can be seen in the background. *John Sharland/Southill Collection*

Garside's locomotive *Ribot* crosses the middle of three narrow gauge level crossings within 100 yards of each other along Billington Road to enter the works. There is hardly any traffic for the man with the 'STOP' board to worry about on 16th February, 1959. *F.A. Blencowe*

Arnold's 40 hp locomotive No. 43, driven by Bob 'Trotter' Turney, sweeps round the sharp bend and across Billington Road with a rake of empties from the washery. *Alan Keef Collection*

Arnold's Billington Road washing plant in 1930 shortly after the transfer of equipment from the Union Street depot. Horses are still being used to haul sand.
Arnold White PLC

A view of Arnold's Billington Road washing plant in 1934. Horse power has been replaced by locomotives. *Joseph Arnold & Sons Ltd*

Arnold's Pratt's Pit in 1930. The building on the skyline is the Leighton Buzzard Urban District Council's 100 ft water tower. *Arnold White PLC*

Arnold's locomotives Nos. 4 and 7 are seen beside Pratt's Pit in adverse weather conditions. Sam Major is ready to flag the locomotives. *Alan Keef Collection*

The LBLR Engine Shed of 1950

Entrance to the Light Railway Works Dept., this building was taken over by Arnold's in 1958 when the LBLR ceased to provide motive power. *John Sharland/Southill Collection*

Reconditioned locomotives stand outside the former LBLR engine shed, by now owned by Arnold's, on 20th September, 1976. No. 41 leading the line with its bonnet raised. *Kevin Lane*

A superb panoramic view of the entire five road layout of Billington Road sidings in 1960 with Arnold's workshops and engine shed on the right. *Alan Keef*

Inside Arnold's palatial engine shed on 8th August, 1968. Twenty Simplexes could be stored here under cover whilst awaiting repairs. This photograph shows a rare view of locomotive No. 44 (*right*) which nobody seems to remember working on the main line. *Chris Daniels*

Arnold's No. 42 stands forlornly inside the workshops on 20th September, 1976. As can be seen 'dead' Simplexes are useful creatures to store things on. *Kevin Lane*

Garside's LBLR No. 10 (MR 10272) awaiting main line duties on 2nd February, 1959. The flag boys comfortable seat is positioned near the radiator. *F.A. Blencowe*

Arnold's No. 7 (MR 3862) bow-framed Simplex shows off some strange optional accessories in Billington Road sidings on 2nd February, 1959. *F.A. Blencowe*

Arnold's No.4 (MR 7201) waits for 12 skips to be detached before taking them onto the high level gantry, August 1968. *Chris Daniels*

Garside's LBLR No. 12 (MR 7932) enters the sidings with empties after crossing Billington Road from the washing plant in 1960. The triangle on the side of the cab was a Garside's identification symbol. *Alan Keef Collection*

The LBLR Engine Sheds of 1919

Arnold's No. 42 (MR 7710) passes in front of the original, corrugated iron, LBLR engine sheds in 1960. Chas Minall, stands on the locomotive, acting as look out and points man.
Alan Keef Collection

Page's Park

Arnold's No. 42 awaits right of way in Page's Park Loops in 1960. The photographer is standing in the position of the old worn out rail lifting barrier. *Alan Keef Collection*

Arnold's 40 hp Simplex No. 43 arrives at Page's Park down the 1 in 69 gradient with a fully loaded train. Note driver 'Trotter's' teddy bear mascot on the cab roof. *Chris Daniels Collection*

Arnold's No. 41 slowly edges skips full of sand into the loops adjacent to Page's Park.
Author's Collection

Garside's 20 hp locomotive No. 16 *Auriole* poses by Page's Park loops in the 1950s.
George Garside (Sand) Co.

Around Stanbridge Road

Arnold's No. 43 leaves the main line to deliver three skips of sand into the restricted siding space of the Leighton Buzzard Concrete Co. on 10th April, 1961.
Sydney Leleux

Arnold's No. 42 climbs up the 1 in 25 gradient of Marley's Bank in 1960 with a full rake of loaded skips. Halfway up the incline an accommodation crossing passes over the the track to connect the two sides of the Marley Roof Tiles factory. *Alan Keef Collection*

Prisoners of War used to work in the sand quarries and at local factories. At Marley Tiles the 'Beware of the Train' sign was written in English, German, Serbo-Croat and Polish. *Kevin Lane*

Leedon Loop

The powerful 3-geared 40 hp locomotive No. 43 is seen at Leedon Loop in 1960. Charlie Gaskin, the LBLR manager, hitches a ride through the tranquillity of the surrounding meadows.
Alan Keef Collection

Clipstone Brook

Arnold's main driver 'Trotter' Turney with his locomotive beside Clipstone Brook on 10th April, 1961.
Sydney Leleux

Garside's No. 12 with its white triangle identification symbol about to cross Vandyke Road in 1960. *Alan Keef Collection*

Arnold's No. 6 pushes a six-skip train off the Chamberlain's Barn branch onto the main line in 1960. The 90 degree Co-op Curve is in the distance. *Alan Keef Collection*

Arnold's No. 6 (MR 7403) in Chamberlain's Barn Quarry on 14th August, 1968. Broomhall's Farm stands precariously close to the edge of the working face. *Sydney Leleux*

Arnold's No. 36 (MR 8756) awaits orders on 19th June, 1975. *Kevin Lane*

New Trees Quarry

From Chamberlain's Barn Quarry another branch line, ¾ mile in length, went over rising meadows to drop sharply into New Trees Quarry. This quarry was rail connected in 1964. Arnold's No. 15 (MR 4803) and No. 34 (MR 9547) begin the stiff climb out of the quarry on 28th July, 1977. By this date, the branch had been lifted and only an internal railway was left taking sand to a loading dock for removal by lorry. *Kevin Lane*

A short steep gradient out of the deep quarry meant that two Simplexes had to be used to haul out the sand. They are now seen gathering speed to take a run up the slope, 28th July, 1977.
Kevin Lane

Arnold's Nos. 15 and 34 still going strong after charging the incline with an eight-skip train, 28th July, 1977. Surely they must reach the top? *Kevin Lane*

Arnold's No. 41 (MR 5839) off the rails in New Trees Quarry on 19th June, 1975. *Kevin Lane*

Arnold's No. 36 (MR 8756) and No. 17 MR 8994 pass their fallen comrade at the top of New Trees Quarry incline on 22nd January, 1976. *Kevin Lane*

Sand being tipped at New Trees Quarry having been hauled out of the pit by Arnold's No. 17 (MR 8994) on 20th September, 1976. *Kevin Lane*

Arnold's No. 15 with one of its last loads, poses by the elevated fuel tank on 23rd November, 1978. *Kevin Lane*

Arnold's Nos. 15 and 34 arrive over the tipping dock at New Trees Quarry on 23rd November, 1978. A few weeks later all railway operations ceased. *Kevin Lane*

The last working. Arnold's No. 15 MR 4803 lies awaiting re-allocation to a new home on 22nd February, 1979. A sad farewell to New Trees Quarry *Kevin Lane*

Along Vandyke Road

Arnold's No. 42 on the main line running beside Vandyke Road on 10th April, 1961. The 40 hp locomotive is returning empty skips to Double Arches. You can almost hear the skips clanking together as the train passes. *Sydney Leleux*

Shenley Hill Road Crossing

Garside's No. 10 (MR 10272) just approaching Shenley Hill Road crossing. The flagman keeps a wary eye open for oncoming traffic. *Alan Keef Collection*

Narrow gauge rails pass Dri-Roof Tiles stacking yard in 1976. The factory was built in the early 1950s and took daily deliveries of sand served by a siding from the main line. *Kevin Lane*

Stonehenge Brickworks main buildings and stacking yard with 2 ft 6 in. gauge trolleys, 28th July, 1977. Each trolley held 1,948 bricks which were stacked to form a rounded arc at the top in order to fit exactly into the steam hardening cylinders known as autoclaves. *Kevin Lane*

Amongst the industries built along the line of the LBLR was Stonehenge Brickworks; this was opened in 1935 under the name of Vandyke Sand/Lime Bricks Ltd but diplomatically changed its name when World War II erupted.

As well as taking thousands of tons of sand each year via the narrow gauge railway, the company also imported huge quantities of lump lime into the works from the nearby Tottenhoe Quarries. This was all delivered by road, despite ready accessibility to the Leighton Buzzard to Dunstable line, Billington Road sidings and the LBLR. If rail transportation was ever considered it would have meant lime travelling along the narrow gauge track as return loads.

A former employee, Arthur Webb, recalls that instead of following his father into the sand pits he joined the workforce at the brickworks in 1943. He was just 14 years old at the time.

For his first year, Arthur was employed as a lorry driver's mate but showed an aptitude for things mechanical and spent the next three years helping to repair and maintain the company lorry fleet. Following his spell in National Service, Arthur returned for a further period at Stonehenge Brickworks looking after ERF lorries which had a top speed of 28 mph and Fodens which travelled at the breakneck speed of 35 mph!

The sand lime brick was a comparatively new invention and was formed by mixing graded sand and lime in precise quantities using (in 1935) the latest German equipment. The mixture was pressurised to 150 psi and cast in to moulds to form the brick which was then stacked onto rail trollies. The trollies were loaded with an arc at the top, each trolley holding 1,948 bricks, and then wheeled into the steam powered hardening cylinder or autoclave. Each autoclave was 6 ft 6 in. in diameter and 60 ft long, over 15,500 bricks could be fitted in the chambers at each 'firing'.

Stonehenge Brickworks was capable of producing over 500,000 bricks per week and Arthur recalls that millions of bricks were transported to Plymouth to help in the rebuilding of that city following World War II.

Redland Ltd took over Stonehenge Brickworks and its associated company Dri-Roof Tiles in 1974.

Personnel at Stonehenge Brickworks in the 1950s included:

Chairman	Mr Blackman
Managing Director	Mr Dicker
Under Manager	Norman Bastow
General Foreman	Guy Jaggard
Steam Engineer	Mr Gunn
Fitter	Bill Gilbert
Blacksmith	Jack Horn
Lorry Drivers	Tommy Yates
	Bert Gaylor
	Tubby Oakman
	Tommy Axston
	Harry Hedges
	Bill Quantrill

A 1934 view of bricks being hand-loaded onto Stonehenge Brickworks' fleet of lorries after removal from the autoclaves. *Arthur Webb Collection*

An eight-wheeler Foden stands in the yard after servicing. The kilns where lump lime was processed can be seen behind the lorry. *Arthur Webb Collection*

A fine view of Stonehenge Brickworks' lorries including ERFs, Fodens and on the extreme right a small Bedford truck. *Arthur Webb Collection*

Arnold's No. 19 (MR 4805) shunts in Dri-Roof Tiles yard on 8th July, 1969. *Mervyn Leah*

Arnold's No. 1 (MR 8683) with a delivery of sand for Dri-Roof Tiles on 24th October, 1974.
Kevin Lane

Arnold's No. 26 (MR 8720) collects empty skips in the works yard on 20th September, 1976.
Kevin Lane

Arnold's No. 19 on the main line returns to Double Arches Quarry for more sand. The old stable block appears mysteriously in the mist. From here horses were led into the quarries to haul the skips in the very early days of the light railway. *Mervyn Leah*

Arnold's No. 12 enters Stonehenge Brickworks siding. All the buildings, with the exception of the stables on the right of the picture, have now gone. Fred Dibnah demolished the chimney in 1985. The track formation still exists to a position just beyond the locomotive. *Chris Daniels*

Arnold's No. 19 (MR 4805) delivering sand to Stonehenge, ready to mix in with lime which has been brought in by lorry and tipped nearby. The old lime kilns are on the right, 12th August, 1968. *Sydney Leleux*

Arnold's stables were erected by prisoners of war in 1919. The structure was built in sandstone obtained from the company's quarries. This building later became part of the Stonehenge Brickworks operations. *Chris Daniels*

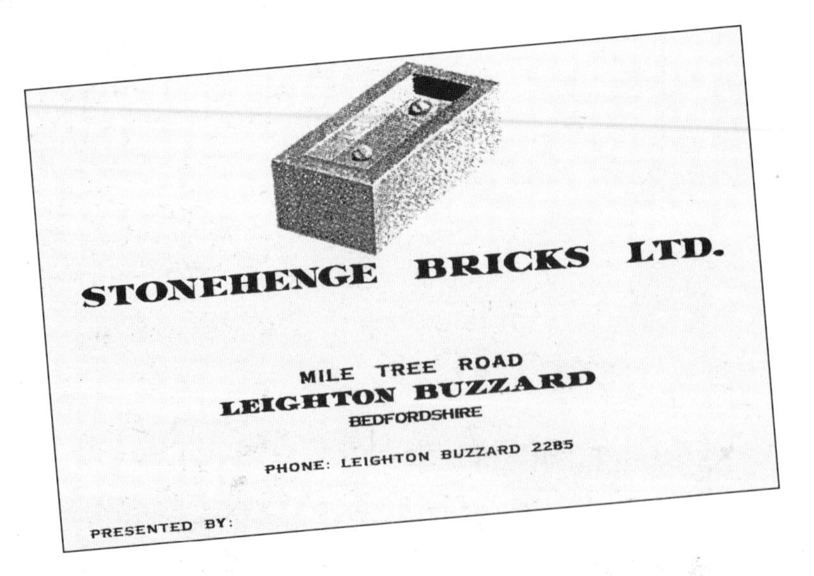

Arnold's No. 1 (MR 8683) passes over Stonehenge Brickworks points on its return journey to Double Arches, 24th October, 1975. *Kevin Lane*

Nine Acre Quarry

Arnold's Nine Acre Quarry (Chance's Pit) *c.* 1935. A steam powered 'navvy' is busy on overburden removal. Under Chance's ownership, much of the output from this quarry was transferred by narrow boat to the Chance Bros & Co. Ltd glassworks in Smethwick.

Joseph Arnold & Sons Ltd

Nine Acre Quarry in 1969. The steam excavator has been replaced and the workings extended right up to the tree line and hedge, compare this with the photograph above.

Joseph Arnold & Sons Ltd

Nine Acre Quarry with Arnold's No. 35 (MR 7126) descending towards the screening plant on 12th April, 1961. *Sydney Leleux*

Arnold's No. 33 (MR 7037) and No. 27 (MR 5863) being loaded by dragline on 12th August, 1969 in Nine Acre Quarry. *Sydney Leleux*

Rogue locomotive Arnold's No. 13 (FH 1917) approaching Stonehenge Brickworks on 8th April, 1954. *Geoffrey Starmer*

Arnold's 40 hp No. 43 going along the section of double track just north of Stonehenge Brickworks. It is believed that this particular section of the LBLR has the longest length of 2 ft gauge industrial double track in the United Kingdom. *Alan Keef*

Arnold's No. 38 (MR 8540) speeds along the higher section of the double track section with empties. The rails are still *in situ* (1997) but buried under a mass of vegetation.
Author's Collection

Beyond the end of the double track , a branch descended into Garside's Munday's Hill Quarry. At this point two Garside's locomotives meet at the junction. No. 31 *Mill Reef* (MR 7371) waits for No. 13 *Arkle* (MR 7108) to clear the main line as it heads a northbound train in December 1979.
Kevin Lane

Two contrasting photographs of No. 13 *Arkle* hard at work shunting and propelling skips on the main line between Munday's Hill Quarry and Garside's Eastern Way washing plant. *Above*: *Arkle* in the frosty depths of winter on 11th January, 1979. *Below*: At the same location *Arkle* shimmers in sylvan surroundings announcing spring has arrived in April 1980.

(Both) Kevin Lane

No. 13 *Arkle* heads towards Munday's Hill Quarry with empties on 5th January, 1978.
Kevin Lane

Garside's No. 34 *Red Rum* MR 7105 leaves Munday's Hill Quarry bound for the company's Eastern Way washing plant in January 1979. *Kevin Lane*

Red Rum with a rake of empties descending into Munday's Hill Quarry on 11th January, 1979.
Kevin Lane

Red Rum continues down the gradient to the bottom of Munday's Hill Quarry. *Arkle* in the distance gives an idea of the scale and depth of the pit, 11th January, 1979. *Kevin Lane*

A close up of the sand strata and formation in Munday's Hill Quarry.
George Garside (Sand) Co.

Ayala MR 7374 with a train about to be loaded at Munday's Hill Quarry.
George Garside (Sand) Co.

Arkle manoeuvres 13 full skips in Munday's Hill Quarry under the watchful gaze of a Ruston Bucyrus 10RB shovel on 5th January, 1978. *Kevin Lane*

George Garside's No. 17 *Damredub* (MR 7036). The 20 hp locomotive like others working in the quarries and along the main line was fitted with a canvas curtain to keep out the worst of inclement weather. *Kevin Lane*

Arkle negotiates the sweeping curve at the bottom of Munday's Hill Quarry. The sleepers are gradually being buried by wind blown sand. *Kevin Lane*

Munday's Hill Quarry produced several different colours of sand. *Damredub* is seen being loaded with yellow sand. The track extended further down the far-reaching face to where pure white sand was exposed under terraces of clay overburden which stretched up to the skyline. *Kevin Lane*

Skips being loaded at Munday's Hill, for *Red Rum* to haul away. Often the Simplex driver also operated the 10RB, loading his own train. It was not unknown for the drivers to leave the brakes off on their trains and then move the skips along for loading by simply pressing down on the sand with the excavator bucket and swinging sideways. It is not recorded if this was authorised practice! *Kevin Lane*

Red Rum heads skips being loaded by 10RB shovel at Munday's Hill Quarry, 5th January, 1978. Above the 20 ft sand face stands a clay band of over 60 ft. *Kevin Lane*

A Ruston Bucyrus loading skips in Munday's Hill Quarry *c.* 1930. The unidentified round-roofed locomotive has yet to be painted with the customary white surrounds on its cab.

George Garside (Sand) Co.

George Garside's MR 7371 *Mill Reef* passes the dragline as it leaves Munday's Hill Quarry in November 1979. There must have been a few anxious moments on the locomotive's journey as the track nearest the photographer looks a bit of a rollercoaster ride. Probably the dragline has been over the track a few times. *Kevin Lane*

Arkle climbs the gradient out of Munday's Hill Quarry in April 1980. The locomotive's round cab roof was a distinctive feature on the railway. *Kevin Lane*

Mill Reef George Garside's No. 31 nears the top of the incline out of Munday's Hill Quarry. The skip in the foreground was fitted with an oil drum and a hand pump in order that the excavators could be refuelled without having to leave the quarry, 20th September, 1976. *Kevin Lane*

Eastern Way Area

Once out of Munday's Hill Quarry it was just a short distance along the main line to the 200 yds-long branch leading to George Garside's Company's drying and grading plant at Eastern Way. *Arkle* is ascending the embankment gaining height to tip the sand down into the hoppers, November 1979. *Kevin Lane*

Red Rum about to leave the grading plant to go back to the quarries, 20th September, 1976. The screening plant at Eastern Way was opened in 1965 replacing installations at Billington Road. The new apparatus was fully automated and processed sand could be directed by conveyor to either a bagging area or directly into lorries. *Kevin Lane*

Arnold's No. 19 (MR 4701) on the main line near Kingsway Farm with a train from Double Arches to Stonehenge on 10th April, 1961. *Sydney Leleux*

Prior to the opening of the Eastern Way plant, Garside's had a tipping dock next to their locomotive shed. This shed once had six roads but this was reduced to two when other buildings became available for locomotive storage. The former shed became a fitters shop for locomotive and excavator repairs, a siding by the old tipping dock was used for redundant locomotives awaiting breaking for spares or scrap. Here No. 15 *Brown Jack* and No. 31 *Team Spirit* stand outside the shed on 14th October, 1972. *Jim Peden*

Arnold's No. 40 about to cross Eastern Way into Double Arches Quarry on 8th June, 1975.
Kevin Lane

Garside's No. 31 *Mill Reef* heads towards the Eastern Way screening plant from Churchways Quarry on 12th May, 1977. *Kevin Lane*

Mill Reef No. 31 gingerly reverses empty skips across Eastern Way on 5th May, 1977. Arnold's drying and bagging buildings were built beside the road just beyond the level crossing.
Kevin Lane

Appearing out of a jungle of shrubs No. 31 *Mill Reef* follows the signs to Leighton Buzzard at Eastern Way on 28th July, 1977.
Kevin Lane

Arnold's No. 40 (MR 7153) going over Eastern Way towards Double Arches Quarry on 5th June, 1975. Some locomotives had an additional window fitted so that the driver could see in all directions. *Kevin Lane*

Arkle crosses Eastern Way heading towards the Churchways washing plant with a full rake of skips. *Kevin Lane*

Double Arches Yards

Arkle continues on its way taking the right-hand branch line into George Garside's quarries in November 1979. A left-hand spur lead into Arnold's Double Arches quarries. A stream marked the boundary between the two company's sand pits. *Kevin Lane*

Garside's No. 26 *Scratch II* slumbers in the sunshine of a late 1950s summer at Double Arches. Close by was the 'Elephant House', Garside's locomotive shed. The clothes strewn over the bonnets and hanging on the brake handle could indicate the driver of the locomotive might be having a quick swim in a nearby flooded pit to cool off. The Simplex was scrapped in 1960. *John Sharland/Southill Collection*

Arnold's No. 42 leaving Double Arches Quarry on 4th January, 1961. The locomotive is just about to be flagged over Eastern Way, train movements were so frequent here that a man was permanently employed to stop the traffic. *Sydney Leleux*

The hustle and bustle of Arnold's constantly busy Double Arches yard on 24th October, 1974. Locomotives arriving include *from left to right,* Arnold's Nos. 33, 36, 16, 26 and 20. Altogether ten locomotives were in daily use with more coming in from other quarries at the end of the day. *Kevin Lane*

In Double Arches Quarry yard Arnold's No. 40 drives over the primary screens on 27th January, 1977. No. 26 was in use as a buffer stop. *Kevin Lane*

Arnold's No. 30 emerges from under the hoppers after collecting its load of screened sand. *Kevin Lane*

Arnold's No. 35 outside the Double Arches shed in March 1976. *Kevin Lane*

Arnold's Nos. 1 and 24 stand outside the Double Arches engine shed on 10th July, 1977. Eleven locomotives could be housed under cover here, on two roads. Other Simplexes were stored overnight under the canopy of the drying shed at the south end of the yard. *Kevin Lane*

Locomotives at rest inside Arnold's engine shed on 5th January, 1978. The engine drivers usually kept to their own engine, swapping only if the Simplex they normally used went into the workshops. *Kevin Lane*

Arnold's No. 35 in the Double Arches workshops on 22nd January, 1976. This single road extension was alongside the main engine shed and was well equipped to carry out minor repairs. Major repairs and overhauls meant the locomotives travelling to the better equipped workshops at Billington Road depot. *Kevin Lane*

Arnold's No. 20 awaits the turn of the handle to start its 20 hp Dorman engine, 20th October, 1974. *Kevin Lane*

Arnold's No. 20 surrounded by a sea of skips, awaits the return of its driver from his lunch break on 24th October, 1974. On the left of the photograph is the washing plant. The buildings in the far distance with the tall chimney are the drying and bagging installations. *Kevin Lane*

Inside Arnold's bagging plant *c.* 1920. There used to be a thriving industry in Leighton Buzzard just making sacks for the sand.
Author's Collection

Arnold's bagging plant at Double Arches in 1940. Sand was dried by spreading on a heated floor fuelled by coke carried from Billington Road sidings in dropside wagons. This was a return load when bagged sand was taken to the exchange sidings. *Joseph Arnold & Sons Ltd*

This photograph shows a belt driven rotary barrel drier which was installed in the plant around 1935. *Joseph Arnold & Sons Ltd*

Abandoned skips greet No. 31 *Mill Reef* in Garside's Double Arches yard, 12th May, 1977. *Kevin Lane*

Arnold's No. 16 MR 4709 looks on as redundant skips are cut up for scrap outside the engine sheds in Double Arches yard on 5th January, 1978.

Kevin Lane

Quarry Locomotives

Despite the introduction of locomotives into the quarries in 1921, horses continued to be used for many years afterwards to haul wagons to the main line connection. Many of the locomotives and bogie wagons used by Arnold's and Garside's had seen active service on the 60 cm gauge War Department Light Railways serving the Western Front during World War I. Surplus railway equipment was repatriated to the UK to be sold to help recover some of the huge cost of the war effort.

The 2½ ton Simplex locomotives with their 20 hp petrol engines were perfect for working in the sand quarries. They had a distinctive bow-shaped channel frame with the engine and gearbox being mounted transversely. The final drive was by roller chain to both axles. The driver sat sideways enabling him to see forwards and backwards with equal ease.

In the mid-1920s straight channel frames were introduced by the Motor Rail and Tramcar Co. of Bedford, followed about 10 years later by heavy deep-sided plate frames. The engines made by Dormans of Staffordshire were converted to diesel from 1935 onwards with big savings in fuel consumption. Both sand companies converted their petrol-engine locomotives to diesel themselves.

Most of the 20 hp quarry locomotives ordered by Arnold's and Garside's were second-hand, all were reconditioned and serviced by Motor Rail before arriving either direct or via 'Petrol Locomotive Hirers', a subsidiary of the company which used to lease locomotives to various contractors for short periods of time and offer them for sale on their return.

There was little difference between the two sand companies' locomotives. Garside's locomotives were supplied by Motor Rail with cabs of the standard design, although some ran cabless throughout their working lives. One side of the cab was open for access to the controls, with a canvas awning to shut out foul weather. The other side behind the driver had an emergency hinged escape hatch in case the engine overturned in a derailment. There were narrow horizontal sliding windows looking front and rear under a ridged roof. Two of Garside's locomotives had curved roofs. Arnold's locomotives were supplied cabless but were fitted with similar cabs home-made in their workshops.

The most distinctive difference between the companies tended to be the design of the bonnets. Here Arnold's chose a ¾ curved bonnet shape covering all the engine with only the bottom edge straight where it rested on the frame. Garside's elected instead to have ½ rounded bonnets with straight sides resting against the cab and frame. All locomotives were painted dark green with white wooden cab window surrounds.

Because of missing works plates it is difficult to produce an accurate record of the Simplexes and other locomotives that worked in the quarries. As far as can be calculated through actual observation or written documentation Arnold's operated 77 locomotives and Garside's a minimum of 67, although some locomotives could have been bought for spares. In addition to the above, 23 locomotives were purchased for the LBLR Company.

Motor Rail also tested some of their production models on the track and at least three, Nos. 8724, 11001 and 21500, can be added to the numbers of locomotives which ran on the line. It is estimated that over 180 locomotives were delivered to all the sand pits in the area, this number must surely have made Leighton Buzzard one of the busiest industrial narrow gauge railway locations in the world.

Arnold's No. 35 with empties preparing to go down into Double Arches South Pit on 5th June, 1975. *Kevin Lane*

Arnold's No. 35 pulling up the gradient out of Double Arches South Pit on 5th June, 1975. Old rail, sleepers and an upturned skip body lie amongst large sandstone rocks along the locomotive's route. *Kevin Lane*

A view of Arnold's Double Arches South Pit on 24th October, 1974. Arnold's No. 26 stands on the wibbly-wobbly track used as a siding where locomotives could wait with empties, whilst another train was being loaded with sand. *Kevin Lane*

The driver of Arnold's No. 8 apologises to the driver of No. 26 for keeping him waiting. No. 8 will continue to Double Arches yard whilst No. 26 will reverse down to the quarry face for loading on 24th October, 1974. *Kevin Lane*

The driver of Arnold's No. 36 (MR 7214) throws the point lever to gain access to Double Arches Middle Pit on 22nd January, 1976. *Kevin Lane*

Arnold's No. 40 (MR 7153) is dwarfed by Double Arches North Pit's dragline on 27th January, 1977. *Kevin Lane*

Arnold's No. 40 leaves North Pit loaded with sand on 27th January, 1977. To reach Double Arches yard the train has to wind its way over the causeway between two flooded pits. Any derailed skips are swiftly removed and are left behind to be gradually buried where they fell.
Kevin Lane

Arnold's No. 35 leaving North Pit with another load of sand bound for Double Arches Yard on 25th March, 1976.
Kevin Lane

From Double Arches yard, George Garside's trackbed branched off to the right and continued for over one mile along a tree lined route, eventually to reach Churchways Quarry. Beyond this lay 'Long Stretch', another rail-connected quarry which suitably marked the end of the line. The photographer has captured the charm of the narrow gauge in this picture as the line meanders through the wooded section of the route. *Alf Fisher*

Arkle emerges through the trees on the Churchways branch on 11th January, 1979. The locomotive is heading for Munday's Hill Quarry with a rake of empty skips. *Kevin Lane*

Narrow gauge charm at Churchways 'Junction'.

Alf Fisher

Arkle stands patiently waiting for skips to be emptied at Churchways on 23rd November, 1978. The sand was tipped down a chute and funnelled onto a conveyor belt system. This raised the sand to a height where the washing process could begin. A final conveyor belt took the sand up to a storage bin. Skips were shunted underneath for loading. *Kevin Lane*

George Garside's *Mill Reef* arrives at Churchways Quarry washing plant with a rake of skips from Munday's Hill on 23rd November, 1978. The sand would be washed here and then taken back down the line again to Eastern Way drying and screening installations. *Kevin Lane*

Tipping sand at Churchways Quarry on 5th January, 1978. *Kevin Lane*

It is hard to believe that this photograph was not taken on the same day as the picture above. The engine driver is the same, however, the railings shown around the chute are by now absent, and electric lamps have appeared instead. *LBNGR Society Archives*

Down in the depths of Churchways Quarry on 12th May, 1977. A rake of skips headed by *Mill Reef* is being loaded. The locomotive will have to reverse its train away from the pit up a considerable gradient to reach the main branch line again. Partially hidden by the cab of the dragline stands *Red Rum*, this locomotive was used as personal transport by the excavator driver to gain access to the quarry. He will take it home again at the end of the working day.

Kevin Lane

No. 31 *Mill Reef* at Churchways with its final load of the day, 5th January, 1978. *Kevin Lane*

No. 31 *Mill Reef* leaves Churchways Quarry on 12th May, 1977. The train travels beside a flooded pit, a good home for pike. Mounds of clay overburden are also a feature of the landscape. The scene has gradually grassed over to leave wagon wheels, skip lids and rails protruding skywards at odd angles, all slowly rusting away with the passing of time. *Kevin Lane*

Ayala crosses a little stream as the locomotive leaves Churchways Quarry to return on its picture postcard journey to Eastern Way, 5th May, 1977. *Kevin Lane*

Beyond Churchways Quarry the track continued on to reach Long Stretch Quarry. When this pit closed a wooden shed was erected over the line. Hidden within the dark confines of this building Garside's kept all their excavator spares and their last petrol locomotive, No. 21 *Festoon*.
Kevin Lane

A wonderful photograph of the 1929-built sole surviving petrol-engined Simplex No. 21 *Festoon*. After hiding away for many years the shy locomotive was finally pushed out of its shed on 14th August, 1968.
Sydney Leleux

An undated photograph of a brand new Motor Rail locomotive under test at Leighton Buzzard.
Chris Daniels Collection

A remote control Motor Rail locomotive on test in 1973. *Motor Rail, Bedford*

When locomotives were beyond economical repair or just worn out through sheer hard work, they were retired to long disused sidings. In the summer months nature swallowed the engines up, only for them to reappear in the winter. Many stood for years in the same spot, occasionally having parts removed but often just rusting away until the day when the scrapman came. Garside's No. 35 *Doutelle* stands forlorn whilst No. 18 *Honeylight* hides in the bushes in this view taken on 5th June, 1975. *Kevin Lane*

The end is nigh, Garside's No. 28 *Flush Royal* cries with a broken heart as she remembers the good old days, 22nd January, 1976. *Kevin Lane*

Garside's No. 15 *Brown Jack* and No. 31 *Team Spirit* have both seen better days. Simplex No. 31 (MR 7371) was saved from the executioner's axe and rose again as *Mill Reef*. *Kevin Lane*

Doom day looms for Garside's No. 30 *Larkspur* at Double Arches dump *c.* 1970. *Kevin Lane*

Lost in the mists of time, Garside's Billington Road scrap sidings on 8th January, 1960.
Sydney Leleux

The last goodbye, Garside's Billington Road scrap sidings, 12th April, 1961. *Sydney Leleux*

After 40 years of loyal service on the Leighton Buzzard Light Railway armoured Simplex No. 3 awaits her appointment with the scrapman, 2nd February, 1959. What a way to go! *F.A. Blencowe*

Protected Simplex No. 5 awaits the gas axe on 2nd February, 1959. The last remains of No. 4 are beyond redemption . . . rest in peace. *F.A. Blencowe*

The last vestige of a once great industrial railway system that saw over 150 locomotives operate over its rails before closure. *Sydney Leleux*

The graveyard crane performs the last rites, 8th January, 1960. *Sydney Leleux*